Cloud Computing
for
Complete Beginners

Building and Scaling High-Performance Web Servers on the Amazon Cloud

Ikram Hawramani

To mother

Contents

Preface

This book is the book I wish I had when I started managing my own web servers for the businesses I own. Due to the complexity of the technologies involved, there is often limitless room for ambiguities and misunderstandings when dealing with servers. You are trying to do tasks that should be simple in theory, but you end up wasting hours and even days trying to make it work. This book helps you avoid that by taking the guesswork out of setting up your web servers on cloud providers, configuring them and scaling them.

This book provides a broad overview of the entire process of building and scaling web servers using a VPS/Cloud provider, while also providing minute step-by-step instructions (with lots of picture and command line examples) on performing each and every important task necessary to get your server(s) going.

If you are completely new to the field, I suggest reading the whole book before you try doing any of it in practice. I find it extremely helpful to first get a broad understanding of a new field (even if I don't understand everything I'm reading) by reading a book or two on it before I actually delve into practicing it.

Note that this book does not teach you programming or website design. It teaches you how to create, manage and scale web servers, and it even shows you how to create a working WordPress installation that you can edit and publish stuff on. It is assumed that you'd use a web developer's services to customize your websites, or that you are a web developer yourself.

1
Choosing and Starting Up Your Server

I will start by assuming that you already have an Amazon.com account. Go to http://aws.amazon.com and sign in to your account.

AWS provides dozens of services. The one we are looking for is EC2 (which stands for Elastic Compute Cloud). After you sign in to AWS, you should see a link to the EC2 section, as shown below. Click on the "EC2" link.

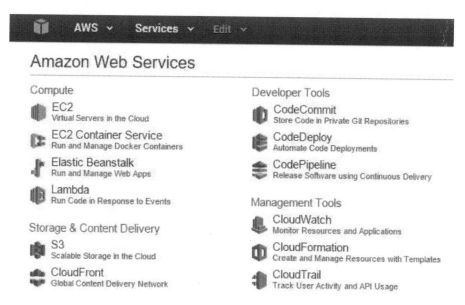

You will enter the EC2 Dashboard. On the left menu, click "Instances" (see picture below). By the time you read this book, some of the design elements may have changed.

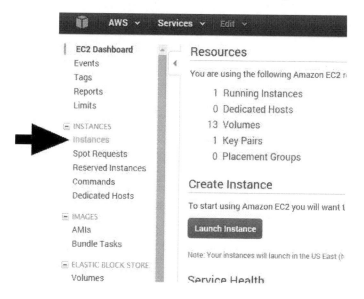

You will be shown a list of your instances (if any). An "instance" is a server, with its own CPU, RAM, and other computing capabilities. You can have as many instances as you need, but thanks to the concept of "virtual hosts" (explained later), you can host as many websites as you like on a single server, which is the smart thing to do in the majority of cases.

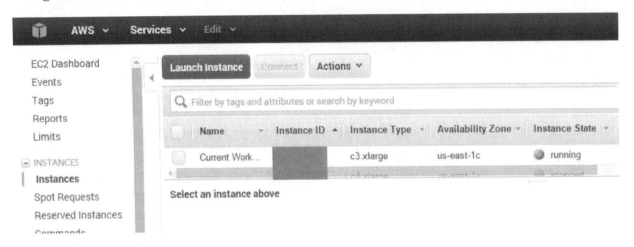

Here you can click "Launch Instance" to create your server.

1.1. Which Instance Type?

I have had good success with a c3.xlarge instance serving 2 million pageviews per month. If you do not expect much traffic, you can start with a t2.small instance (costing $18.7/month). Use ec2instances.info to browse the various instance types, their characteristics and their hourly and monthly costs. Look at the "Linux On Demand Cost", this is the cost that applies to the instance you are going to build.

Looking at ec2instances.info, you will see that some instances have "Storage" (see picture below), while others are "EBS only". The more expensive instances come with what Amazon calls "ephemeral storage", this is what the "Storage" column refers to. Ephemeral storage consists of hard drives or SSDs that come with the instance and that can only be used for temporary data storage, since the data on them is wiped whenever the instance is rebooted.

The cheaper instances do not come with ephemeral storage. This is not a big deal since ephemeral storage is just a bonus and not necessary.

What you will use for permanent data storage (for storing your website's files and server programs) is an EBS volume, which can be a hard drive or an SSD (solid-state drive). SSDs are far superior to hard drives for server applications, as they are orders of magnitude faster. For this reason I recommend using SSDs unless you have a very good reason for using hard drives.

When creating a new instance, you will be prompted to create an EBS volume, and that is when I will speak more about this.

Click "Launch Instance" on the "Instances" page shown earlier. You will be shown the following page:

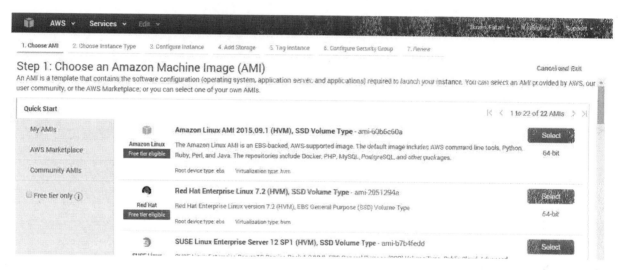

On this page, you select the type of server you want to build. On the left, you can see a link to the "AWS Marketplace". On that page, you can choose pre-built servers that have all the necessary server programs already installed for particular web server types. For example, you can search for "wordpress" and you will be shown various options for pre-built WordPress servers. I do not suggest using pre-built servers in general because they are either hard or impossible to update (due to the pre-built servers relying on various hard-coded mechanisms that do not work with Linux's update software), or they cost extra money hourly beyond the usual AWS charges. Therefore if you look for pre-build instances on the AWS Marketplace, make sure you take note of any additional charges.

For the purposes of this book, we will choose the Ubuntu option. Scroll down until you see Ubuntu 64-bit, then click "Select".

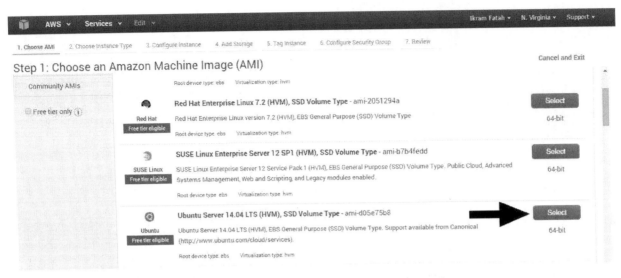

Ubuntu Server has the largest user base of any Linux distribution, which makes it a safe and reliable option. Use the 64-bit variant since there is generally no good reason to use a 32-bit server.

After selecting the server distribution, you will be prompted to select the instance type. I will select t2.small, then click "Next: Configure Instance Details" to go to the next step.

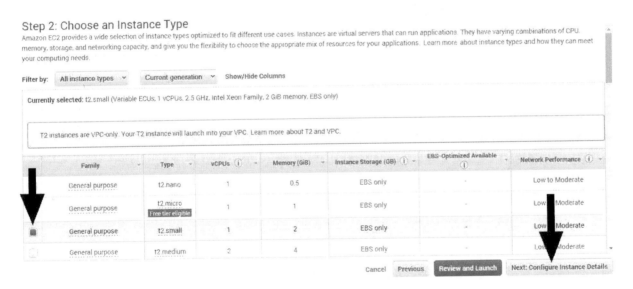

You will reach Step 3, "Configure Instance Details". You do not need to make any changes to this step unless you have a reason to. Click "Next: Add Storage" to reach the next step.

Below is an image of the storage page:

Step 4: Add Storage

Your instance will be launched with the following storage device settings. You can attach additional EBS volumes and instance store volumes to your instance, or edit the settings of the root volume. You can also attach additional EBS volumes after launching an instance, but not instance store volumes. Learn more about storage options in Amazon EC2.

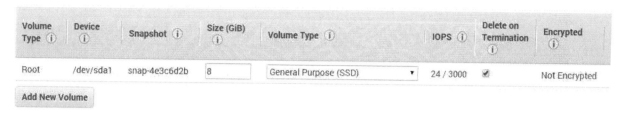

Volume Type ⓘ	Device ⓘ	Snapshot ⓘ	Size (GiB) ⓘ	Volume Type ⓘ	IOPS ⓘ	Delete on Termination ⓘ	Encrypted ⓘ
Root	/dev/sda1	snap-4e3c6d2b	8	General Purpose (SSD) ▾	24 / 3000	☑	Not Encrypted

Add New Volume

Choose the "Size" in gigabytes. Note that the size determines the speed of the disk (the IOPS, for "input-output operations per second"). I suggest starting with a size of 20 gigabytes, which gives you 60 IOPS. If in the future your storage needs increase, you can always add a new disk to your instance. Choose "General Purpose (SSD)" for "Volume Type" unless you have a good reason to choose otherwise.

Note that AWS charges you by the gigabyte for your SSD. The price is quite low, $0.10 per gigabyte, meaning that a 20 gigabyte disk will cost you $2 per month (this is in addition to the instance's monthly cost).

Go to the next step, which is the tagging step where you can add tags to your instance. Tags are labels or notes that help you describe the instance for your own future reference. There is no need to add tags unless you are going to be managing lots of instances and need to categorize them. Go to the next step.

This step is the "Configure Security Group" page, which is quite important, since the wrong setting will make your server unreachable to the outside world:

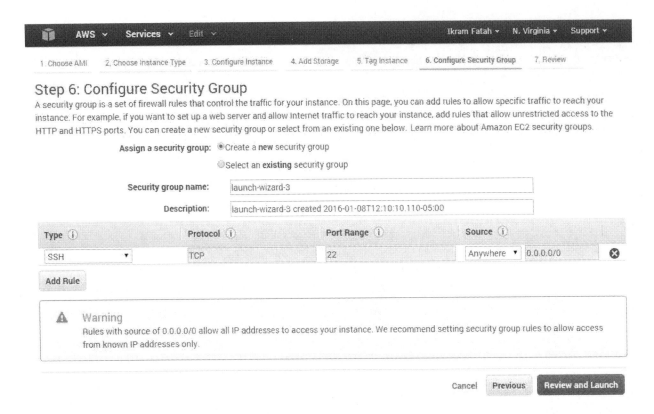

Click "Add Rule" (near the bottom left of the image above), and in the "Type" combo box choose "HTTP". The rest of the fields will be filled out automatically for you. Then click "Add Rule" again and choose "HTTPS", again the rest of the details will be filled out for you. The HTTPS rule allows access to SSL-encrypted webpages. If none of your websites use SSL, then you do not need it. If you don't know what SSL is, skip the HTTPS step.

Once you are done, click "Review and Launch". You will see the page below. Ignore the warnings. Since you are launching a web server, it *has* to be open to the world.

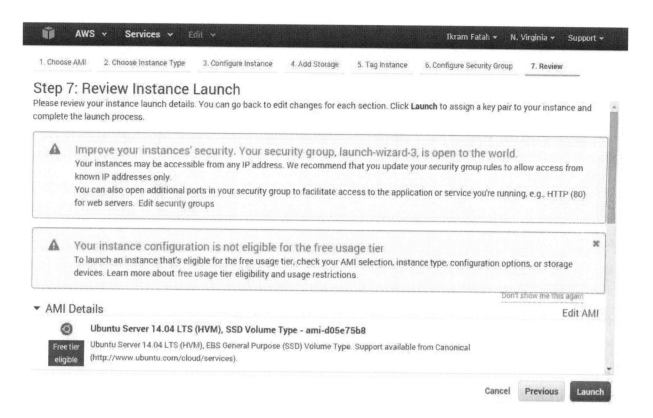

Review the details of your instance, then click "Launch". You will be prompted to select or create a "key pair". This is the security mechanism you will use to security access your instance remotely (instead of using a password). Give the key pair a friendly name, then click "Download Key Pair" to download the key file to your computer. This file will be the "key" that you will use to access your server, therefore make sure you do not lose it. Never share this key file with others, as it will enable them to access your server and do whatever they like to it.

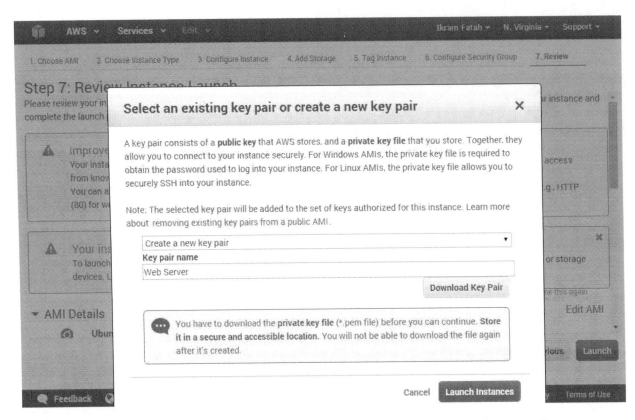

Once you are done downloading the key pair, click "Launch Instance". You will get a message saying that your instance is launching. Click on the new instance's ID to view its launch progress.

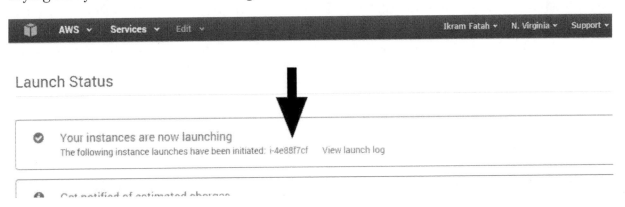

You will be taken to the instances page, with a filter active that only shows the new instance on the list (so don't get scared if you have other instances and you do not see them):

It generally takes a few minutes for an instance to become fully operational after launch. Some types of instances take longer to launch than others. Once you see "2/2 checks passed" in the "Status Checks" column, it means you instance is probably online, though sometimes you will need to wait a minute or two after this to be able to reach the instance.

2
Entering Your Cloud Server

To enter your server, the first thing you need to do is get the server's public address, which you can find out on the "Instances" page. If you have multiple instances, you need to click on the check box to the very left of the instance row in order to show its information.

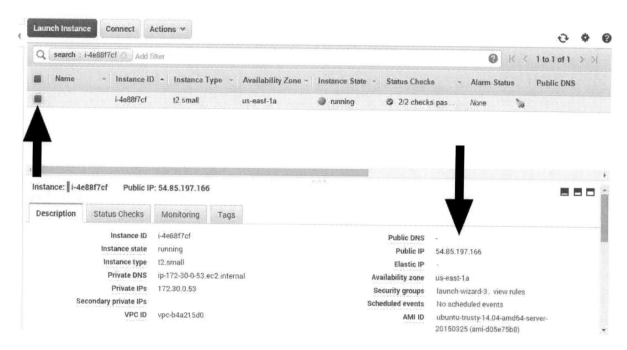

In this book, I will use the Linux command line to interact with the server. If you have never used the command line (where you interact with a computer using text only, no mouse), don't be afraid. I will show you everything you need to know.

To enter the server, you will use SSH (which stands for Secure Shell), which is a secure way of accessing a server remotely. If you use Windows as your local machine, you will use a Windows tool called PuTTY to enter your Linux server, as I will explain below.

2.1. Logging in from Linux
If the local computer you use (i.e. your home or work compuer) is a Linux computer, you'd enter the following command in therminal to SSH into your server:

ssh -i */path/*my-key-pair.pem ubuntu@54.85.197.166

The default username for Ubuntu is "ubuntu", thus you are signing into 54.85.197.166 as the user "ubuntu".

2.2. Logging in from Windows

If you are on Windows, download PuTTY (http://putty.org). Make sure to download both putty.exe and puttygen.exe, as you will need both.

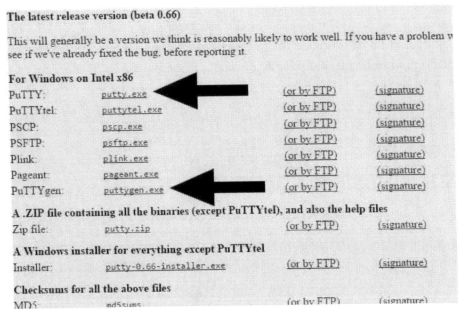

First, you will convert the key file (that you downloaded right before launching your instance) into a format that PuTTY can use. To do this, open up puttygen.exe. Make sure "SSH-2 RSA" is selected at the bottom, then click "Load":

In the window that opens, first change the file type combo box to "All Files", otherwise PuTTYGen won't see the ".pem" file that contains your key. Browse to the location of your key file then click the "Open" button:

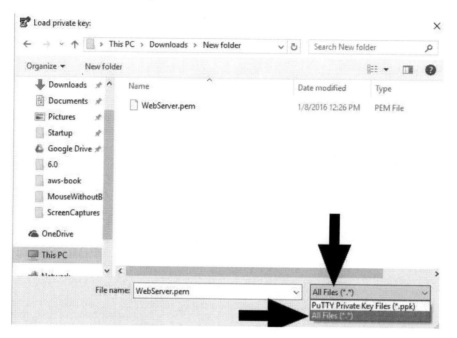

Click "Save private key". The program will ask if you are sure you want to save the key without a passphrase, click "Yes". Putting a passphrase on your key will be more secure, but it can be quite inconvenient. PuTTYGen will create a PPK file for you that you can use with PuTTY. Save this file somewhere safe.

Now, open putty.exe and enter your instance's IP address. Keep the port as 22, which is the default SSH port. You may notice that the IP in the picture below is different from the one shown earlier. This is because I rebooted the server. Every time you reboot the server, AWS assigns a different IP address to it. Later I will show how to get a static IP address, which is essential for a web server.

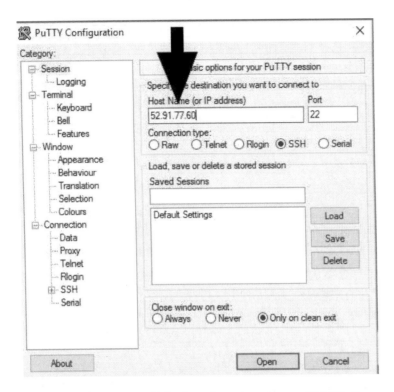

On the left menu, click the plus sign nexto "SSH", then click "Auth":

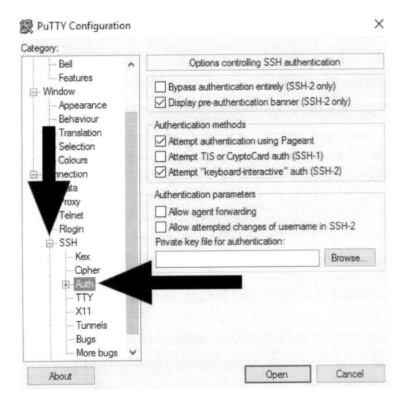

Click the "Browse" button (also shown above), and select your PPK file. Then click "Session" on the left menu to go back to PuTTY's main page.

Type a friendly name in the "Saved Sessions" box, then click "Save" so that PuTTY saves your login details, so that you do not have to go through these steps gain.

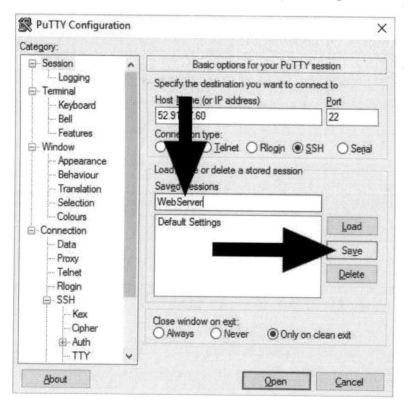

Now, if I close and open PuTTY again, the name "WebServer" will appear in the white area that currently only contains "Default Settings". You will have to click it, then click "Load" (above "Save") to load your server's details.

Click "Open" to start your session. You will get a security warning if it is your first time connecting to your server. Click "Yes". You will see a login screen, type "ubuntu" as your username then press Enter:

You will be logged into the server without the need for a password, as the key file you selected in PuTTY is a (safer) substitute for a password.

The first thing to do after logging into your Ubuntu server is to do an update. To check for updates, type:

sudo apt-get update

...then press enter. This only checks for updates, without applying them. To apply the updates, type:

sudo apt-get upgrade

This does not upgrade Ubuntu itself to a new version (since you want to stay with the current version of Ubuntu offered on AWS, rather than trying newer and more experimental ones), even though the command seems to suggest that it might do a system upgrade. It actually only upgrades the various software packages and applies various bug and security fixes.

During the "upgrade" command, you may get prompted for various things. Generally you'd type "y" (for "yes") and press enter to agree to do the things that the update command wants to do. However, sometimes you may be asked if you want to keep the local version of a file or if you want to download the newer one, generally you should choose to keep the local version (otherwise some things may stop working), unless you have a reason to download the newer file.

3
Installing and Configuring Your Server Software

I will use a common software stack (a group of different tools that work together for a particular purpose) known as the LAMP stack (which stands for Linux, Apache, MySQL and PHP).

I will use the WordPress CMS for website building examples. Many people wrongly think that WordPress is a simple blogging service. They are thinking of wordpress.com, which is built on the WordPress software, but is only one example of a service built on WordPress. Through using the WordPress CMS, you can create your own alternatives to wordpress.com and any other website or service you can think of. The WordPress CMS makes life so much simpler for website builders by taking care of all the boring details—things like securely logging into the website back-end, creating users, connecting to a database and storing information on it, sending newsletters, blogging, etc.

There are good alternatives to WordPress, such as Joomla and Django. WordPress and Joomla are written in PHP (the "P" in LAMP), while Django is written in Python. The language a CMS is written in makes a difference, since you'd use that language to add any programmatic features to your website, or to customize the user experience.

There is no need to worry too much about the language however, since unlike human langauges, once you learn a computer language and become good at it, you can learn your way around the essential parts of another language in a matter of minutes.

3.1. Installing LAMP

Use the following two commands to install LAMP:

```
sudo apt-get install tasksel

sudo tasksel install lamp-server
```

After the second command, you will be prompted to type a MySQL root password. Type a password and make sure you don't forget it as you will likely need it in the future.

In Ubuntu, whenever you perform an important and potentially unsafe command, you need to prepend "sudo" to its beginning in order for it to be carried out, otherwise you will be denied permission. This is an important feature that helps avoid doing accidental damage to your server.

3.2. Testing Your Install

Do you remember your server's IP address? If not, you can check it out on your EC2 Instances page. To test that your server is up and running, type your server's IP address in a browser, such as in Google Chrome (shown below).

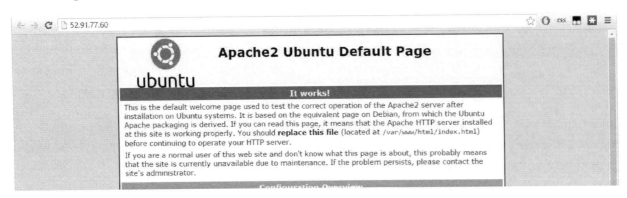

If your server is working properly, you should get an Ubuntu/Apache default welcome page.

The web page you saw above is actually a file on your server. You can generally find it at /var/www/html/index.html. The Apache server considers any "index.html" file in this folder as the "root" of your website, i.e. as its main page and starting point, unless you tell it to do things otherwise.

3.3. Installing WordPress

There are various ways of installing WordPress. Here I will show the manual, reliable way of doing it.

Step 1. Go to your document root directory (/var/www/html). "Directory" is the Linux word for what is commonly called a "folder" on Windows.

```
cd /var/www/html
```

Step 2. Download the latest zipped version of WordPress.

```
sudo wget http://wordpress.org/latest.tar.gz
```

wget is the standard Linux download utility. The link shown above will always contain the latest version of WordPress (the developers update the file as the new versions are released without changing the link).

Step 3. Extract the WordPress download into its own directory.

```
sudo tar xzvf latest.tar.gz
```

This will create a directory named "wordpress" in your root directory that will contain your WordPress files, thus you will end up with:

```
/var/www/html/wordpress
```

Step 4. You won't need the zipped version of WordPress anymore that you downloaded in Step 2 (since you have unzipped it). Run the rm command to remove the unnecessary file:

```
sudo rm latest.tar.gz
```

Step 5. Do an update check and install two software packages that will be necessary for running WordPress properly. You may get a [Y/n] prompt during the installation, type "y" and press Enter.

```
sudo apt-get update
```

```
sudo apt-get install php5-gd libssh2-php
```

Step 6. You will now create the necessary changes to the MySQL database to make it ready for WordPress. WordPress doesn't store its data (things like posts) in files, it stores them in a database for quick access, for this reason you need functioning database software on your site to run WordPress. Fortunately, MySQL is a free and powerful database management system, for this reason you will not be needing anything more for your database needs.

Log into the MySQL "server" (i.e. the MySQL program) running on your server. The wording can be confusing. Your Ubuntu installation is a "server", while the Apache program running inside it is also a "server", and of course MySQL is also a server. A server is any program that stays up and waits for other programs to make requests to it. That are various other servers running on your server, but these are enough to know about, at least at your current stage.

```
sudo mysql -u root -p
```

You will be prompted for your MySQL root password (which you set earlier in the chapter, type it in and press Enter.

Run the following five statements (pressing Enter after each line). You can keep everything as it is, except for the "password", which should be changed to something a bit less easy to guess.

```
CREATE DATABASE wordpress;

CREATE USER wordpressuser@localhost IDENTIFIED BY 'password';

GRANT ALL PRIVILEGES ON wordpress.* TO wordpressuser@localhost;

FLUSH PRIVILEGES;

EXIT;
```

The first statement above creates a database called "wordpress". This database will being storing almost all of your WordPress settings and data.

The second statement creates a user called "wordpressuser" (a MySQL server can have multiple users and you do not want to be using the root user for WordPress tasks, since that makes it so much easier for hackers to destroy your database). On the third statement you give the user full control over the "wordpress" database's contents.

The fourth statement "flushes" the MySQL privileges, meaning that MySQL will be made aware of the changes we made in statement three without having to restart the MySQL server.

The final statement exits you out of the MySQL server and takes you back to the Ubuntu command line.

3.4. Configuring WordPress

The next step is to create the WordPress configuration file and make a few necessary changes to it. Go into the WordPress directory:

```
cd /var/www/html/wordpress
```

WordPress provides a sample configuration file (wp-config-sample.php) to get you going. Copy this file and name it wp-config.php to turn it into the real configuration file.

```
sudo cp wp-config-sample.php wp-config.php
```

Now, open wp-config.php for editing. There are various text editors that come with Linux. Personally I prefer Vim, but beginners will enjoy nano more. To open the file, type:

```
sudo nano wp-config.php
```

Use your arrow keys and the rest of the keys on your keyboard like you'd do on a Windows text editor. Here are the lines you'd need to change:

```
define('DB_NAME', 'wordpress');

define('DB_USER', 'wordpressuser');

define('DB_PASSWORD', 'password');
```

The "wordpress" in the first line above is the database name that we chose in the first line of your MySQL statements. The second and third lines come from the second line of your MySQL statements.

There are eight lines of code starting with "define('AUTH_KEY..." and ending with "define('NONCE_SALT...". These are important definitions required for the safety of your installation. Go to https://api.wordpress.org/secret-key/1.1/salt/ to generate these eight lines automatically and copy and paste them into your wp-config.php file instead of trying to come up with your own random strings. Thus, you start with the following:

```
define('AUTH_KEY',      'put your unique phrase here');
```

```
define('SECURE_AUTH_KEY',  'put your unique phrase here');

define('LOGGED_IN_KEY',   'put your unique phrase here');

define('NONCE_KEY',       'put your unique phrase here');

define('AUTH_SALT',       'put your unique phrase here');

define('SECURE_AUTH_SALT', 'put your unique phrase here');

define('LOGGED_IN_SALT',  'put your unique phrase here');

define('NONCE_SALT',      'put your unique phrase here');
```

Then, you delete all of these lines, go to the link provided above, and copy and paste everything from there.

3.5. Setting Up a .htaccess File

WordPress uses a type of Apache configuration file called a *.htaccess* file that controls the way Apache processes particular directories. Your WordPress installation needs a *.htaccess* for certain tasks, such as setting up pretty permalinks. For this reason, it is important to create this file. To do so, first visit https://codex.wordpress.org/htaccess and at the top, in the Basic WP section, you will see the default WordPress .htaccess file that you can use for your own install.

Navigate to */var/www/html/wordpress*. Run the following command to create an empty *.htaccess* file:

```
sudo touch .htaccess
```

Change the file ownership so that Apache can modify the file when necessary:

```
sudo chown www-data:www-data .htaccess
```

Then edit the file to paste the default *.htaccess* contents into it:

```
sudo nano .htaccess
```

If you are using PuTTY, you can just copy the content of the *.htaccess* file from the website, open up the *.htaccess* file for editing, then right-click on the PuTTY window to paste it into there.

3.6. Telling Apache to use Your WordPress Installation

Find your Apache installation directory, usually it is */etc/apache2*. In there, find the */sites-available* directory, and edit the file found in there (named something with *default* in it and ending in ".conf"). You can use nano again for editing, making sure to use "sudo" before it (*sudo nano file.conf*), otherwise you will be denied permission.

Here is the line that needs to be changed:

```
DocumentRoot /var/www/html
```

Change it to:

```
DocumentRoot /var/www/html/wordpress
```

This tells Apache to look for your website's main page in the *wordpress* directory.

Save the file and exit nano. Then restart Apache using the following command in the command line:

```
sudo service apache2 restart
```

Merely editing the Apache configuration files will not apply your changes. Apache needs to be restarted so that it reloads the configuration files. When starting or restarting Apache, you may get various notices and error messages (as shown below). As long as it says [OK] on the last line, you can safely ignore the messages.

```
ubuntu@ip-172-30-0-53:/var/www/html$ sudo service apache2 restart
sudo: unable to resolve host ip-172-30-0-53
 * Restarting web server apache2
AH00557: apache2: apr_sockaddr_info_get() failed for ip-172-30-0-53
AH00558: apache2: Could not reliably determine the server's fully qualified doma
in name, using 127.0.0.1. Set the 'ServerName' directive globally to suppress th
is message
                                                                          [ OK ]
```

3.7. Testing and Debugging the WordPress Installation

Go to your server's ip address in your web browser. If everything worked out correctly, you'd see a WordPress page. If not, you may see a "Server Error 500" page. If you see an error page, the first thing to do is check the Apache error log (generally found in /var/log/apache2/error.log). There are many ways of opening an error log to look at it. One of them is to use *less*, a Linux utility.

```
less /var/log/apache2/error.log
```

The *error.log* file will be opened in *less* for you too look at. You want to to see the end of the file, which will contain the latest error reports. For this reason press shift+g on your keyboard (to send a capital G signal to *less*), which tells *less* to jump to the bottom of the file. If you do not look at the bottom, you will probably see a ton of irrelevant error reports. You do not want to read them all to see what is wrong. Just jump to the bottom. There you will see Apache's troubles.

Here is an example of an error report in *error.log* caused by a typo in the *wp-config.php* file which we dealt with a little while back.

[Sat Feb 06 14:51:17.813539 2016] [:error] [pid 30978] [client 50.153.214.232:22223] PHP Parse error: syntax error, unexpected '/' in /var/www/html/wordpress/wp-config.php on line 21

The report helpfully tells us that it is a syntax error on line 21 of the *wp-config.php* file. Let's go take a look:

```
sudo nano -c /var/www/html/wordpress/wp-config.php
```

Note that I am using *nano* with the -c argument, this tells *nano* to show line numbers, which is important at the moment, since we want to find line 21. Use the arrow keys to go down the file, *nano* will continue telling you which line you are on.

This is what I have on lines 20 and 21:

```
/** The name of the database for

WordPress */ define('DB_NAME', 'wordpress');
```

The above two lines should instead be:

```
/** The name of the database for WordPress */

define('DB_NAME', 'wordpress');
```

The first line is a "block" comment", and nothing should come after it on the same line.

After correcting that, I try going to my server IP again and it still doesn't load WordPress. This is what the Apache error log says this time:

```
[Mon Feb 08 13:35:46.385943 2016] [:error] [pid 10819] [client 50.153.213.60:22538] PHP Parse error:
syntax error, unexpected end of file in /var/www/html/wordpress/wp-config.php on line 80
```

When I look at *wp-config.php* again, I see that there is actually no line 80. The file ends at an empty line 79 (showing 78 and 79 below):

```
/** Sets up WordPress vars and included files. */ require_once(ABSPATH . 'wp-settings.php')

```

To an experienced developer, the error is obvious. Line 78 lacks a semicolon at the end, so to PHP the file does not end properly. I will add a semicolon and delete the unnecessary empty line:

```
/** Sets up WordPress vars and included files. */ require_once(ABSPATH . 'wp-settings.php');
```

And that's it! This time when I go to my server's IP address, this is what I see:

Welcome

Welcome to the famous five-minute WordPress installation process! Just fill in the information below and you'll be on your way to using the most extendable and powerful personal publishing platform in the world.

Information needed

Please provide the following information. Don't worry, you can always change these settings later.

Site Title	[_____]
Username	[_____] ✳
	Usernames can have only alphanumeric characters, spaces, underscores, hyphens, periods, and the @ symbol.
Password	xj((TqwoYAMKW0lnbD ⊕ ∅ Hide
	Strong
	Important: You will need this password to log in. Please store it in a secure location.
Your Email	[_____] ✳
	Double-check your email address before continuing.
Search Engine Visibility	☐ Discourage search engines from indexing this site
	It is up to search engines to honor this request.

[Install WordPress]

Fill out the form and press "Install WordPress". The information you enter here can be changed later, so do not worry about getting everything perfect on the form. You will next see the success page:

After logging in, you will see the WordPress dashboard. You are ready to start building your website(s). You can have multiple WordPress installations on the same server, each hosting a different website, as I will show later.

3.8. Configuring WordPress's File Permissions

Apache should be made the owner of the directory that contains your WordPress installations, otherwise you will run into "permission denied" errors. Go to your *www* directory:

```
cd /var/www
```

Run this command to make Apache the owner of the *html* directory and everything below it, which includes your WordPress installation.

```
sudo chown www-data:www-data -R *
```

The name of the Apache *user* is *www-data*. *chown* is the Linux utility used for changing file permissions.

Next, run the following two commands inside the same directory to give the directories and files proper read/write permission settings:

```
sudo find . -type d -exec chmod 755 {} \;
```

```
sudo find . -type f -exec chmod 644 {} \;
```

3.9. Making WordPress Updateable

By default, WordPress cannot update itself or download and install plugins and themes unless you provide it with a way of doing this. The easiest way is to open *wp-config.php* and add this on a new line at the end:

```
define('FS_METHOD', 'direct');
```

This is good enough to get you going with a test site, but it is not a perfect permanent solution, since it gives WordPress too much power over your server, potentially leading to security issues. It is better to set up FTP or SSH2 access for WordPress to improve your security. Google "wordpress ssh2 updates" to find tutorials on doing this.

After logging into your WordPress site, you may see an update notification as shown below:

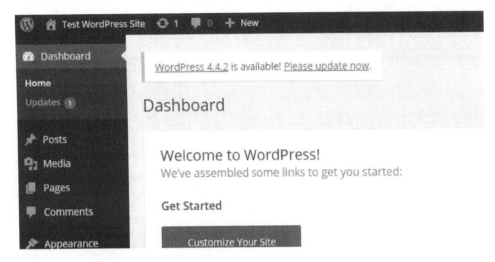

It is important to always keep your WordPress sites up-to-date, since updates often contain important security fixes. Click "Please update now". On the next page, click "Update Now". Once the update finishes, you will see a welcome page for the new version of WordPress. Sometimes you may also be prompted to update your database, if so, go through with that.

Welcome to WordPress 4.4.2

Thank you for updating! WordPress 4.4.2 makes your site more c

| What's New | Credits | Freedoms |

4

Setting Up a Static IP Address for Your Server

By default, AWS gives your server a temporary IP address that lets you enter your server and do the necessary installation procedures. This IP address is only good as long as your instance is running. Stopping the instance or rebooting it will cause the IP address to be lost a new one assigned. Therefore on a production server, it is important to have a static IP address, otherwise your sites will become inaccessible after a reboot.

Amazon calls its static IP service "Elastic IPs" and offers them free for running instances. If you stop your instance, the IP address becomes unattached to your instance, but you do not lose it. After starting your instance again, you can re-associate the IP address with your instance so that your sites continue to be accessible.

If you stop (shut down) your instance, your account will start accruing charges at a rate of $0.005 per hour (3-4 dollars per month) for reserving your Elastic IP. Once you start your instance again and associate the Elastic IP with it again, your account will stop accruing this charge.

To get your Elastic IP, log in to your AWS console and find the "Elastic IPs" link in the "Network & Security" section:

NETWORK & SECURITY
   Security Groups
   Elastic IPs
   Placement Groups
   Key Pairs
   Network Interfaces

On the page that opens, click "Allocate New Address" at the top:

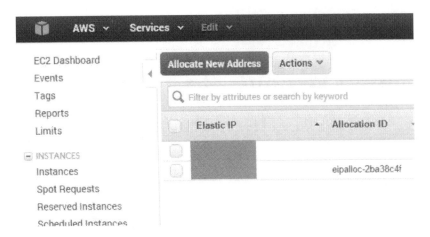

Depending on the type of instances running on your account, you may get the following dialog box, which asks you where to allocate the address. If you have a T2 instance, for instance, you'd choose "VPC", since T2 instances are VPC instances. For most other instances, you'd choose EC2, unless during the instance creation process you specified that the instance be launched into a VPC.

When you are ready, click "Yes, Allocate". You will get a success message, then you will see your IP in the list of IP addresses. The one that was assigned to me was 52.86.4.143:

You now need to associate the IP address with your instance. To do so, right-click on the IP address, then click "Associate Address":

4. Setting Up a Static IP Address for Your Server

In the dialog box that opens, click inside the "Instance" box and Amazon is nice enough to give you a list of available instances that you can associate the IP with without having to type anything in the box:

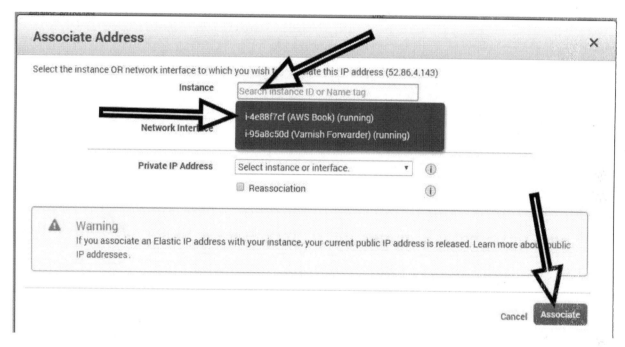

I see my instance's name (AWS Book) in the list, so I click on it.

Next, click "Associate" on the dialog box.

When you go back to the Instances page, you will see that the instance's IP address is now a link, rather than plain text. Clicking on the link will take you to the Elastic IPs page.

When you go back to the Instances page, you will see that the instance's IP address is now a link, rather than plain text. Clicking on the link will take you to the Elastic IPs page.

Now that your server has a static IP address, its old public address will stop working and the next time you log in via SSH you'd need to use the new static IP.

4.1. Fixing WordPress after an IP Change

After your server's IP changes, your WordPress installation may start malfunctioning, loading like this:

Test WordPress Site

Just another WordPress site

Hello world!

Welcome to WordPress. This is your first post. Edit or delete it, then start writing!

Author ikramPosted on February 8, 20161 Comment on Hello world! Edit "Hello world!"
Search for: [Search ...]   [Search]

What this means is that your browser is failing to load the WordPress style files. This happens because WordPress is still referencing your old IP address in its internals, trying to load part of your site through the new IP and part of it through the old IP.

To fix, this go into MySQL to update WordPress's idea about your site's IP address. Type the following command in the command line:

```
mysql -u wordpressuser wordpress -p
```

This tells MySQL to log in as the *wordpressuser* and to select the *wordpress* database. The *-p* tells MySQL to prompt you to enter a password. If you omit the *-p*, you will be denied access. Enter the password for the *wordpressuser* which you set earlier in this book and press Enter.

If you are using PuTTY, you can copy the password (if you have it saved in a file), then right click on the PuTTY window to paste it. PuTTY will not give any indication that a paste has occurred since this is a password prompt and Linux does not show any feedback when typing passwords.

Once you are inside the MySQL command line, type the following command to update your IP in the wordpress database:

```
update wp_options set option_value = "http://NEWIP" where option_value = "http://OLDIP";
```

This updates every instance of the old IP in the database, which normally exists only on two rows of the *wp_options* table, as seen by typing the command below:

```
mysql> select * from wp_options where option_value = "http://52.86.4.143"
    -> ;
+-----------+-------------+---------------------+----------+
| option_id | option_name | option_value        | autoload |
+-----------+-------------+---------------------+----------+
|         1 | siteurl     | http://52.86.4.143  | yes      |
|         2 | home        | http://52.86.4.143  | yes      |
+-----------+-------------+---------------------+----------+
```

In the next chapter I will show a simpler way of updating these two rows by adding two lines to a WordPress theme file.

5

Setting up a Domain Name and Configuring WordPress to Use it

I am including this short chapter for completeness, for readers who expect this book to walk them through the entire site-building process, which necessarily includes acquiring and configuring a domain name, so that your website can be accessed via example.com rather than an IP address.

To get a domain, first you need to buy it (though you can test a domain without buying it as I explain in the next section) from a "domain registrar". There are seemingly endless companies that sell domains, including even Google. Sign up with such a company, find the domain you like and buy it. Then, visit your domain's "DNS Settings Page". Different registrars have different ways of referring to this page, search the registrar's knowledge base or wiki for "change dns settings" to find out where you can find this page.

Once on that page, choose to add an "A" record to your domain. Below is an example of doing this on some registrar's website:

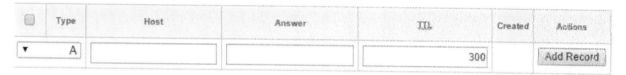

All that you need to do is paste your server's static IP address in the "Answer" box, then click "Add Record". The "Host" should remain empty, unless you wish your site to be accessed as www.example.com rather than example.com. In that case, type www in the box. If you'd like your site to be accessed via both methods, you'd add two records, one with an empty "Host" and the other with "www" in the "Host" box.

Once you add the record, there is a "propagation" period during which the domain will not work. This can last up to 24 hours. Go to www.whatsmydns.net and type your domain in the box. Once all the results show your server's IP, you know propagation is complete or practically complete.

5.1. Testing a Domain without Buying It

You can make your home computer think that a particular domain refers to a particular IP, even if to the outside world this is not the case. This can be done by editing the *hosts* file, which on Windows exists on *C:\Windows\System32\drivers\etc\hosts*, while on Mac it exists on */private/etc/hosts*. On Linux, you'd need to edit the */etc/hosts* file.

If your server IP is 52.86.4.143 and you want your computer to connect the domain *example.com* with this IP, put this line in the *hosts* file:

52.86.4.143 example.com

Now, when you type "example.com" in your browser, the browser will connect to the server at 52.86.4.143 to request the website. If it doesn't load, close and open your browser again, or try it in another browser.

In this way you can test a non-existent domain on your local computer, either for development or convenience. You can even set up domains that can't even exist on the internet. For example, add this line to the hosts file:

52.86.4.143 a.a

Now, if you type a.a in your browser, you will be taken to your server/website.

5.2. Updating WordPress to Use the Domain

At the end of the previous chapter I showed a way of updating the *wordpress* database in MySQL to make WordPress work properly with the new static IP. Now that we have a domain, we may have to do this again if WordPress is not loading properly. I will show the easier way of doing it.

Open your wp-config.php file:

sudo nano /var/www/html/wordpress/wp-config.php

At the very bottom of the file, temporarily add these two lines:

update_option('siteurl','http://example.com');

update_option('home','http://example.com');

These two lines tell WordPress to update its idea of what your site's domain name is, telling it it is http://example.com. Make sure to include the "http://".

Once you add those two lines and save the file, go to your WordPress site once. You have to visit your site once to run the *update_option* functions in the *wp-config.php* file. Once is enough. Go back to *wp-config.php* and remove the two lines from the bottom. Leaving them in there would cause WordPress to make two unnecessary database calls every time someone visits any page on your site, which can cause slow down your site without contributing anything.

6
Creating and Attaching New Disk Drives

AWS makes it very easy to add new drives to your server. Note that in general it is better to use one large SSD disk on AWS rather than multiple small ones. Due to the way the AWS infrastructure is designed, one large disk will probably get you better speeds than multiple smaller ones

But if you need extra space and you do not want to migrate your data to a large disk, then attaching a new disk is the best option you have. One reason why you'd want to use an attached disk is that you want to create backups that are not always accessible from your server. You'd attach the disk, put your backups on it, then detach it and perhaps copy it. This way you'd have a safe copy of your data stored on AWS that cannot be harmed if hackers break into your server.

To create a new disk drive (also called a "volume"), on the EC2 dashboard, click the "Volumes" link on the left menu:

Once on the Volumes page, click "Create Volume".

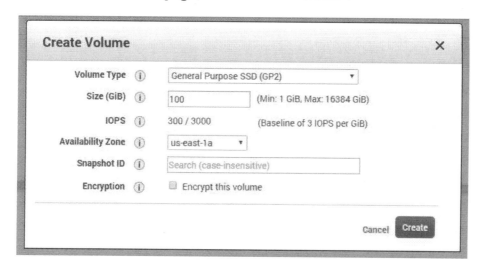

Leave the Volume Type as "General Purpose SSD" unless you have a good reason to change it. The size of the disk affects the amount of bandwidth available to it (and thus how fast data can

be transferred to and from it), so a higher disk space would get you a faster disk, but it would also cost more.

Important: Make sure to choose the same Availability Zone for the volume as you chose for your instance, otherwise your disk will end up in a datacenter miles away from where your instance is.

Leave the Snapshot ID and Encryption boxes alone, then click "Create". You will see the new disk on the list of volumes on the Volumes page:

The "Name" field above is blank. You may click on it and change it to another name so that later you can remember the purpose of the disk.

The disk's State is "available" after creation, which means it is not attached to anything yet. To attach it to your instance, right-click on the disk's Name (or Volume ID, or any other of the properties) and click "Attach Volume".

A dialog box opens up. Click inside the Instance box so that Amazon gives you a list of your running instances. Then click the name of your instance.

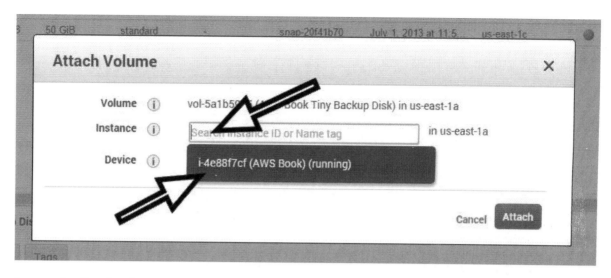

Leave the Device box as it is, then click "Attach".

You will see a loading icon next to your disk's name while the attachment is in progress.

You are not done yet! You need to get into your server and "mount" the disk. No need to wait for the loading icon to disappear, since once in the server you can check if the disk is attached, and that gives you more real-time data.

Log into your server and type the following command:

```
lsblk
```

Here is what this command outputs on my server:

```
NAME       MAJ:MIN RM SIZE RO TYPE MOUNTPOINT
xvda       202:0    0  20G  0 disk
└─xvda1    202:1    0  20G  0 part /
xvdf       202:80   0  10G  0 disk
```

The new disk is listed as "xvdf", you can recognize it by the fact that its size is 10G. There are only two disks on the server, the line in the middle, where it says "part" for the TYPE is a partition of the main disk. You can partition a disk into multiple partitions for some advanced uses. In this case, there is only one partition that is the same size as the disk, which means the partition takes up the entire disk.

The name "xvdf" has nothing to do with the name shown in the Device box on Amazon. This is because some operating systems have their own naming schemes and they don't care about

Amazon's opinion of how the device should be named. Ubuntu is such an OS. This is not a problem, just an inconvenience where you have to run the *lsblk* command to find out your new device's name.

Another way of seeing your new attached disk is to run this command:

ls /dev

This command lists the contents of the /dev ("devices") directory. You will see the disk near the very end. If you attach another disk to your instance, it will be shown under "xvdf" and will be called "xvdg", and so on down the alphabet for additional disks.

```
ttyS24      vcsa6
ttyS25      vcsa7
ttyS26      vga_arbiter
ttyS27      xen
ttyS28      xvda
ttyS29      xvda1
ttyS3       xvdf
ttyS30      zero
```

NOTE: The more expensive EC2 instances come with "ephemeral" storage, which are disks that you will see listed on the page when you do an *ls /dev*. The disks are for temporary data storage. You can use them like normally attached disks, except that once the instance is turned off or rebooted, all the data in these disks will be wiped. They are for storing temporary files and should never be used to store anything important.

To make the disk usable by your instance, you will "format" it, then you will "mount" it. First, run this command:

sudo mkfs.ext4 /dev/xvdf

Note that if your device name is something other than "xvdf", you would change the above command to reflect that.

Next, decide upon the directory where you want the disk to be placed. For example, I will create a directory called /aws_backups in the server's root (top) directory:

sudo mkdir /aws_backups

Next, I will mount the disk on the directory:

sudo mount /dev/xvdf /aws_backups/

Now, when I run the df -h command, the system confirms that the disk has been mounted on /aws_backups (see bottom line):

```
Filesystem      Size  Used Avail Use% Mounted on
udev            996M   12K  996M   1% /dev
tmpfs           201M  336K  200M   1% /run
/dev/xvda1       20G  1.1G   18G   6% /
none            4.0K     0  4.0K   0% /sys/fs/cgroup
none            5.0M     0  5.0M   0% /run/lock
none           1001M     0 1001M   0% /run/shm
none            100M     0  100M   0% /run/user
/dev/xvdf       9.8G   23M  9.2G   1% /aws_backups
```

The disk shows up as less then 10G because when you format a disk, some disk space is used for storing metadata about the file system's structure. This is not "lost" space, it is necessary data that has to exist for the disk to function.

The disk is now ready for use.

6.1. Detaching a Disk

To safely detach a volume, first type the following command, where "xvdf" is the name of your volume:

```
umount -d /dev/xvdf
```

Note that the command is *umount*, NOT *unmount*.

Once you unmount the disk, the directory on which it was mounted continues to live on. If you copy a file into it, the directory will act like any normal directory on the main disk and the data will be stored on the main disk. If you put some stuff into the directory, then mount the disk on it again, the original contents become invisible until you unmount the disk.

Next, on the EC2 Dashboard, on the Volumes page, right click on the disk and click "Detach Volume":

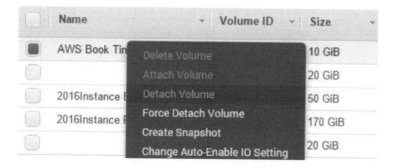

You will get a confirmation dialog box. Click "Yes, Detach". After a short wait the volume will be detached and available for reattachment to the same instance or another instance. You may also choose to keep it detached until you need to use the disk again.

7

Hosting Multiple Websites on Your Server

The Apache web server supports having multiple websites hosted on the same server/IP address. If you have two domains, example1.com and example2.com, when a user types either of these in their browser, Apache is able to see the request and make different decisions based on whether the user requested example.com or example2.com.

There is no limit on the number of websites you can set up with Apache on your instance. Some web hosting companies put hundreds of websites on a single server.

Note that the DNS records for both domains should point to the same IP address; your server's static IP.

To start, use the instructions from chapter 3 to create a new WordPress installation in a new directory under /var/www/html. You may also clone your present WordPress installation instead of creating a fresh install. This is not as simple as just copying the files over. The next chapter deals with cloning WordPress installations. Below, I'm assuming you are creating a new WordPress installation.

In chapter 3 we installed WordPress in a directory called *wordpress*. You can create a directory with your second domain's name as your second installation:

```
cd /var/www/html
sudo mkdir example2.com
```

Assuming you already set up example.com for your */var/www/html/wordpress* installation, here we are creating */var/www/html/example2.com* for the second installation. You do not need to use your site's name for the directory name, but doing so makes it easier to identify.

7.1. Setting up Virtual Hosts

You will set up a "virtual host" for each one of your domains. In chapter 3, you already set up a virtual host for your main installation by editing the */etc/apache2/sites-available/000-default.conf* file. You will now disable this one and create two new ones, each file's name having your domain name in it for ease of use.

First, copy the default configuration file:

```
cd /etc/apache2/sites-available
sudo cp 000-default.conf example.com.conf
```

Now, open up the *example.com.conf* file for editing:

```
sudo nano example.com.conf
```

Find this line in the file:

```
DocumentRoot /var/www/html/wordpress
```

And add these two lines above it:

```
ServerName example.com
ServerAlias www.example.com
```

That's all for your first domain. For your second domain, copy the first domain's configuration file into the same directory and open it up for editing:

```
sudo cp example.com.conf example2.com.conf
sudo nano example2.com.conf
```

Repeat the same steps to add the ServerName and ServerAlias directives to the file, this time specifying example2.com instead of example.com, AND also specifying your second domain's new *DocumentRoot* (its installation directory) by editing the *DocumentRoot* line as well:

```
ServerName example2.com
ServerAlias www.example2.com
DocumentRoot /var/www/html/example2.com
```

Once you are done, run these two commands to enable your domains:

```
sudo a2ensite example.com.conf
sudo a2ensite example2.com.conf
```

You can also disable the default virtualhost to prevent your server from loading anything when someone types your server's IP address in their browser. You could also create a third installation and update the default virtual host's *DocumentRoot* to point to it, so that when you or someone types the server's IP address in a browser, they see the third installation.

Assuming you want to disable the default virtual host, use these commands:

```
cd /etc/apache2/sites-enabled
sudo a2dissite 000-default.conf
```

Finally, to make your changes live, restart Apache:

```
sudo service apache2 restart
```

8

Speeding Up Your Websites with the Varnish Accelerator

The Varnish HTTP Accelerator, which henceforth I will refer to as Varnish, is a "caching" engine that allows a server to handle 10-100 times more traffic than it would normally be able to. Without Varnish, when someone requests your home page, Apache has to launch various tasks to build and process the page's PHP code and database connections. With Varnish, this process only happens once, because it saves the results of all these processes as a static file, so that the next time someone visits your home page, they are served the static file by Varnish without any reference to Apache or PHP.

8.1. Installing Varnish

Type this command on the command line:

```
sudo apt-get install varnish
```

Once the installation is done, Varnish will be automatically started.

8.2. Configuring the Varnish Daemon

Varnish will not do anything after the initial installation, unless you tell it to by routing requests to your website through it.

First, stop Varnish:

```
sudo service varnish stop
```

Now, open up the Varnish daemon settings file, which controls the basic settings for Varnish:

```
sudo nano /etc/default/varnish
```

Find the line that looks like this:

```
DAEMON_OPTS="-a :6081 \
       -T localhost:6082 \
       -f /etc/varnish/default.vcl \
       -S /etc/varnish/secret \
       -s malloc,256m"
```

The first line tells Varnish which "port" to "listen" on. For requests to your website to go through Varnish, this port has to be port 80, which is currently used by Apache. Set it to 80 and we will take care of Apache later:

DAEMON_OPTS="-a :80 \

The next important line is:

```
-s malloc,256m"
```

This tells Varnish to store the cached webpages in memory (in RAM), rather than on disk, and it gives it a limit of 256 megabytes, meaning that Varnish will use up to 256 megabytes of RAM to store cached webpages, but no more.

You may also tell Varnish to store its cache on disk rather than in memory. This is necessary when using Varnish to cache massive websites where the cache can gets as large as dozens of gigabytes and it becomes impractical to store that much in memory.

Here is the line I use on one of my servers, which gives Varnish 14 gigabytes of disk space for storing cached webpages:

```
-s file,/mnt/varnish_store.bin,14G
```

The "/mnt/varnish_store.bin" is the path to the file where Varnish will store its cached webpages. This file doesn't have to exist. You can specify any existing directory and Varnish will create the file inside it.

8.3. Editing the Varnish VCL File

Varnish's settings for how it handles your site(s) is stored in another file. It is found in /etc/varnish/default.vcl. By default, the *default.vcl* file has only four lines of active configuration:

```
backend default {
    .host = "127.0.0.1";
    .port = "8080";
}
```

The .*host* setting tells Varnish where Apache is located, is it on the same server or a different server? The IP address 127.0.01 refers to the server itself, which tells Varnish that Apache is on the same server as itself.

The .*port* setting tells Varnish where to connect to Apache internally. This is different from the port setting of the previous section.

We will need to set Apache to use the 8080 port so that Varnish can find it and connect to it. We will do that in a later section.

Everything else you see in the file has been "commented out" by preceding the lines with a # so that they do not do anything until you remove the preceding #.

To tell Varnish to store a cached webpage for one hour before it requests a new version from Apache, you'd use the following lines:

```
sub vcl_fetch {
    set beresp.ttl = 1h;
}
```

That is TTL, not TT1.

You might have two websites, one of which is updated every ten minutes, while another is updated only once every a few days. In such a case, you can tell Varnish to use different settings for each website. Below, I am telling Varnish to store cached webpages for example.com for two days, while telling it to store cached webpages for example2.com for only 10 minutes. If there is a third website, it will use the default *1h* (one hour) setting on the second line.

```
sub vcl_fetch {
  set beresp.ttl = 1h;
  if (req.http.host ~ "(www\.)?(example)\.com") {
    set beresp.ttl = 2d;
  }

  if (req.http.host ~ "(www\.)?(example2)\.com") {
    set beresp.ttl = 10m;
  }
}
```

It is also important to add the following lines to your vcl_fetch settings so that Varnish does not cache error pages that happen when Apache temporarily goes down or fails to deliver a page. If Varnish caches such error pages, then the next time someone tries to visit the page, Varnish serves them the cached error page, which is a pretty bad thing, since the actual page might be accessible by then while your site's visitors keep seeing an old error page.

To prevent such a situation, add these three lines to the *vcl_fetch* function:

```
if ( beresp.status >= 500 ) {
    set beresp.ttl = 0s;
}
```

The first line is saying if the webpage has a status of 500 or more (which happens when Apache is down, or when there is a syntax error in your PHP code), do the following. The second line is what Varnish will do, which is keep the webpage in cache for 0 seconds, meaning that the next time someone tries to visit that webpage, Varnish will request it again from Apache, and hopefully this time is Apache is up, or the PHP syntax error has been corrected. If not, Varnish will continue requesting the webpage again and again from Apache as people visit the webpage, until Varnish gets a proper webpage, at which point it will cache it like any normal webpage.

We will also need to make some changes to the *vcl_recv*. If you are worried about how to put it all together, don't worry, I will present the completed file at the end. If you wish a particular website, such as example.com, to never be cached, add the following three lines to *vcl_recv* function:

```
if (req.http.host ~ "(www\.)?(example)\.com") {
    return(pass);
}
```

If you care about RSS feeds, you may want to tell Varnish to not cache RSS feeds so that your users can always get the latest updates through RSS. Here is how:

```
if ( req.url ~ "/my/feed/url" ) {
    return(pass);
}
```

The above applies to all of your websites, as it doesn't specify a domain name.

It is generally a bad idea to server cached pages to logged in users (suc has yourself when you are on the WordPress Dashboard). To prevent that, use the following three lines:

```
if ( req.http.cookie ~ "wordpress_logged_in") {
    return( pass );
}
```

You will also want to drop cookies that users send to your site unless they are on the login or admin area, since they shouldn't be doing that.

```
if (! ( req.url ~ "wp-(login|admin)" ) ) {
    unset req.http.cookie;
}
```

To speed up your website, Varnish supports compression. This can be configured using the following lines on the *vcl_recv* function:

```
if ( req.http.Accept-Encoding ~ "gzip" ) {
    # If the browser supports it, we'll use gzip.
    set req.http.Accept-Encoding = "gzip";
}

else if ( req.http.Accept-Encoding ~ "deflate" ) {
    # Next, try deflate if it is supported.
    set req.http.Accept-Encoding = "deflate";
}

else {
    # Unknown algorithm. Remove it and send unencoded.
    unset req.http.Accept-Encoding;
}
```

8.4. The Complete VCL File

Below is the file that puts all the above settings together. Note that Varnish has many more settings than these. This is a barebones file to get you going, even though it will function perfectly and will vastly speed up your site's load times.

Note that since the settings prevent Varnish from caching pages for logged in users, if you are logged into your WordPress site, you will not be able to see how fast the pages are loading with Varnish, since you are skipping the cache. To test the cache, open an incognito window (in Chrome) and load your site there. The first time it loads, it may not load from the cache if it is not already cached. Refresh the page and the next time you will see it load from the Varnish cache.

```
backend default {
    .host = "127.0.0.1";
    .port = "8080";
}

sub vcl_fetch {
  set beresp.ttl = 1h;
  if (req.http.host ~ "(www\.)?(example)\.com") {
    set beresp.ttl = 2d;
  }

  if (req.http.host ~ "(www\.)?(example2)\.com") {
    set beresp.ttl = 10m;
  }
}

sub vcl_recv {
    # Do NOT cache this site
    if (req.http.host ~ "(www\.)?(example)\.com") {
        return(pass);
    }

    # Do NOT cache this feed
    if ( req.url ~ "/my/feed/url" ) {
        return(pass);
    }

    # Do NOT cache pages for logged-in users
    if ( req.http.cookie ~ "wordpress_logged_in") {
        return( pass );
    }
    # DROP unwanted cookies
    if ( ! ( req.url ~ "wp-(login|admin)" ) ) {
        unset req.http.cookie;
    }

    # Set up compression
    if ( req.http.Accept-Encoding ~ "gzip" ) {
```

```
        # If the browser supports it, we'll use gzip.
        set req.http.Accept-Encoding = "gzip";
    }
    else if ( req.http.Accept-Encoding ~ "deflate" ) {
        # Next, try deflate if it is supported.
        set req.http.Accept-Encoding = "deflate";
    }
    else {
        # Unknown algorithm. Remove it and send unencoded.
        unset req.http.Accept-Encoding;
    }
}
```

8.5. Changing the Apache Port

By default, Apache listens on port 80, this is the default HTTP port. When someone visits a page on your website, their browser connects to port 80 and requests the page from whatever program on the server which happens to be "listening" on this port.

Since we want to use the Varnish cache, we need put Varnish on port 80 and move Apache to a different port (since two programs cannot listen on the same port). In the previous section we told Varnish that Apache listens on port 8080, therefore we will change the Apache configuration files so that this becomes true. You can use any port for Apache that you want, making sure to update the */etc/varnish/default.vcl* file to reflect the Apache port.

To change the Apache port, open up the *ports.conf* file:

```
sudo vim /etc/apache2/ports.conf
```

Change the top *Listen* directive to 8080 rather than 80:

```
Listen 8080
```

You can ignore the rest of the lines on the file.

8.6. Setting the Virtual Hosts to Use the New Apache Port

After changing the Apache port, the virtual hosts you set up in Chapter 7 have to be updated. This is a simple process, you just update one line on each file of the */etc/apache2/sites-available/* directory.

Open up each file. This is the first line of the file:

```
<VirtualHost *:80>
```

Update it to:

```
<VirtualHost *:8080>
```

Save the files, then restart Apache:

sudo service apache2 restart

Then start Varnish:

sudo service varnish start

8.7. Testing that Varnish Works

Type your site's domain name or IP address in Firefox. Once it opens up, right-click on an empty area of the page and click "Inspect Element":

The Firefox Inspector will open up. Click on the "Network" tab:

Click on "Reload":

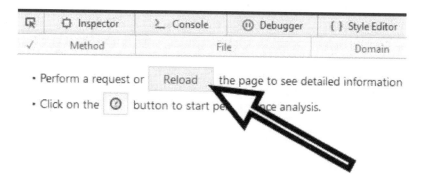

The webpage will reload and you will see a list of your site's file and the speed by which they loaded. Scroll to the top to the first row, which refers to the main web page. Below we can see that the page loaded in 252 milliseconds.

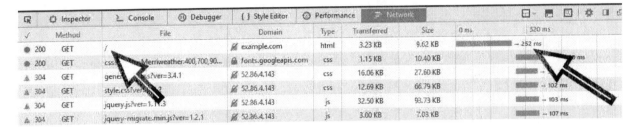

Click on the first row. This will open the Headers information pane on the right:

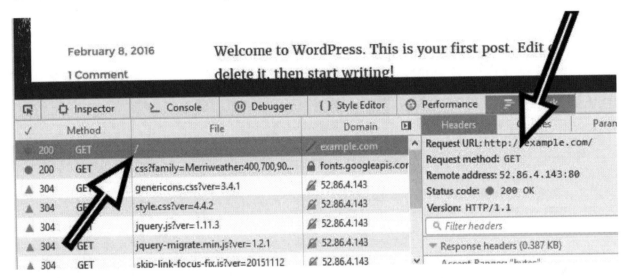

In the "Filter headers" search box, type "varnish":

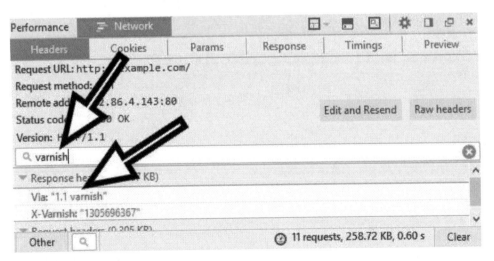

The search will return two lines about Varnish, which is all the confirmation you need that Varnish is serving the page.

What if you want to know whether Varnish served a cached page or fetched the page from Apache rather than the cache? To do, you will need to add the following function to your /etc/varnish/default.vcl file:

```
sub vcl_deliver {
    if(obj.hits > 0) {
        set resp.http.X-Varnish-Cache = "HIT ("+obj.hits+")";
    } else {
        set resp.http.X-Varnish-Cache = "MISS";
    }
}
```

After adding that, restart Varnish. Now, when you reload the page and search for "varnish" again, you will see the following:

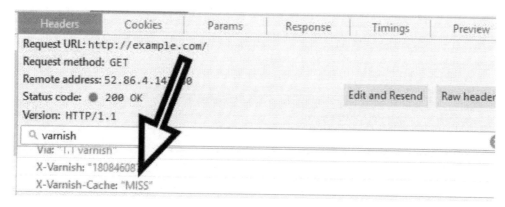

It says "MISS", which means the page was not loaded from the cache. This is because it is the first time I visited the site after restarting Varnish. The Varnish cache is cleared every time Varnish is restarted. When I reload the page, this is what I see:

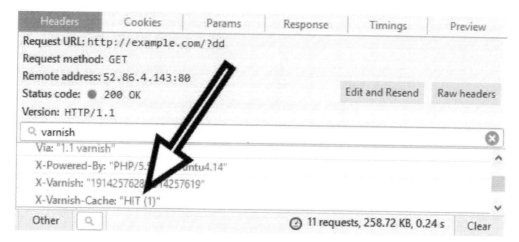

"HIT" means the page was loaded from cache. The number referrs to the number of times the page was loaded from cache (how many "hits" the cache received for that particular page).

If it keeps saying "MISS", you probably have this in your vcl_fetch function, which unsurprisingly prevents Varnish from caching the site:

```
# Do NOT cache this site
if (req.http.host ~ "(www\.)?(example)\.com") {
    return(pass);
}
```

In Chapter 11 I show how to use Varnish to do load balancing, so that you can have multiple servers serving the same site, which is something you need to do for very high-traffic sites or sites that occasionally get large traffic spikes.

9
Creating a Swap File

A swap file is a file that the operating system uses as an extension to its memory (its RAM), so that during conditions where the server is about to run out of memory, it can continue to function (albeit slowly) instead of crashing. The swap file is also used to offload rarely used data from memory to free up more memory for applications that actually need it.

EC2 instances do not come with swap set up, it is something you will have to do manually.

First, use the following command to create a 4 gigabyte file named *swapfile* in your server's root directory:

sudo fallocate -l 4G /swapfile

Run the following command so that only the root user can access the file:

sudo chmod 600 /swapfile

Next, turn the file into a swap file using the following command:

sudo mkswap /swapfile

And finally, tell your operating system to use the swap file as its swap file:

sudo swapon /swapfile

You can check whether the swap file is properly set up by running the following command:

sudo swapon -s

```
ubuntu@ip-172-30-0-53:/var/www/html$ sudo swapon -s
sudo: unable to resolve host ip-172-30-0-53
Filename                          Type        Size      Used   Priority
/swapfile                         file        4194300   0      -1
```

10

Monitoring Performance and Auto-Restarting Apache after Crashes

10.1. Monitoring CPU and Memory Usage

My first go-to tool when trying to gauge the state of a server is the *top* utility. Type "top" on the command line and press enter to open it up.

```
top - 18:31:49 up 22:28,  1 user,  load average: 0.00, 0.01, 0.05
Tasks: 104 total,   1 running, 103 sleeping,   0 stopped,   0 zombie
%Cpu(s):  0.0 us,  0.3 sy,  0.0 ni, 99.7 id,  0.0 wa,  0.0 hi,  0.0 si,  0.0 st
KiB Mem:   2048484 total,    802008 used,   1246476 free,     74548 buffers
KiB Swap:  4194300 total,         0 used,   4194300 free.    548436 cached Mem

  PID USER      PR  NI    VIRT    RES    SHR S %CPU %MEM     TIME+ COMMAND
    1 root      20   0   36812   6184   1520 S  0.0  0.3   0:01.40 init
    2 root      20   0       0      0      0 S  0.0  0.0   0:00.00 kthreadd
    3 root      20   0       0      0      0 S  0.0  0.0   0:00.00 ksoftirqd/0
    4 root      20   0       0      0      0 S  0.0  0.0   0:00.00 kworker/0:0
    5 root       0 -20       0      0      0 S  0.0  0.0   0:00.00 kworker/0:0H
    6 root      20   0       0      0      0 S  0.0  0.0   0:00.01 kworker/u30+
    7 root      20   0       0      0      0 S  0.0  0.0   0:00.24 rcu_sched
    8 root      20   0       0      0      0 S  0.0  0.0   0:00.72 rcuos/0
```

The first things to look at are the load averages on the top right. You will see three numbers, which show the load averages for the past 1, 5 and 15 minutes respectively. The load averages usually reflect CPU usages, but not always. They represent whatever resource limitation that happens to be causing processes to queue, whether it is CPU, disk usage or something else. On a dual-core CPU, a load of 2 would mean that both CPUs are being fully used. The load averages are not something to worry about if your site is having decent load times, and if the load average divided by the number of CPU cores is not too high.

To see CPU usage for each CPU separately on a multi-core instance, press the "1" key on your keyboard. On a t2.small instance pressing "1" doesn't show any additional information, since there is only one CPU core:

```
top - 18:33:49 up 22:30,  1 user,  load average: 0.00, 0.01, 0.05
Tasks: 104 total,   1 running, 103 sleeping,   0 stopped,   0 zombie
%Cpu0  :  0.0 us,  0.0 sy,  0.0 ni,100.0 id,  0.0 wa,  0.0 hi,  0.0 si,  0.0 st
KiB Mem:   2048484 total,    802008 used,   1246476 free,     74548 buffers
KiB Swap:  4194300 total,         0 used,   4194300 free.    548436 cached Mem
```

But on a 4-core c4.xlarge instance, here is how the top command breaks down the statistics by core:

```
top - 18:35:46 up 4 days, 18:58,  1 user,  load average: 3.27, 3.80, 4.36
Tasks: 146 total,   1 running, 144 sleeping,   0 stopped,   1 zombie
%Cpu0  : 16.5 us,   2.7 sy,  0.0 ni, 80.8 id,  0.0 wa,  0.0 hi,  0.0 si,  0.0 st
%Cpu1  : 36.7 us,   5.1 sy,  0.0 ni, 58.2 id,  0.0 wa,  0.0 hi,  0.0 si,  0.0 st
%Cpu2  : 50.7 us,   3.3 sy,  0.0 ni, 45.4 id,  0.3 wa,  0.0 hi,  0.3 si,  0.0 st
%Cpu3  : 62.2 us,   6.0 sy,  0.0 ni, 31.1 id,  0.0 wa,  0.0 hi,  0.7 si,  0.0 st
KiB Mem:   7659540 total,  6786512 used,   873028 free,    69768 buffers
KiB Swap:  8388604 total,   544016 used,  7844588 free.  1775588 cached Mem
```

The *top* command shines when you reduce its update interval to milliseconds. To do so, while inside the *top* utility, press the "s" key on your keyboard, then type 0.1, which tells *top* to update every 100 milliseconds, then press Enter.

```
KiB Swap:  4194300 total,
Change delay from 3.0 to 0.1
```

By default *top* sorts the processes by CPU usage. On a web server I often find it more helpful to sort them by memory usage. To do so, hold down they Shift key then press the "greater than" key on your keyboard, which is generally on the left of the question mark key. Here is what the result looks like on a busy web server:

```
top - 18:43:28 up 4 days, 19:05,  1 user,  load average: 6.65, 4.91, 4.58
Tasks: 155 total,   9 running, 146 sleeping,   0 stopped,   0 zombie
%Cpu(s): 90.5 us,   9.5 sy,  0.0 ni,  0.0 id,  0.0 wa,  0.0 hi,  0.0 si,  0.0 st
KiB Mem:   7659540 total,  5968028 used,  1691512 free,    37344 buffers
KiB Swap:  8388604 total,   544012 used,  7844592 free.   796868 cached Mem

  PID USER       PR  NI    VIRT    RES    SHR S  %CPU %MEM     TIME+ COMMAND
27367 mysql      20   0 7895224 4.000g   4828 S  38.2 54.8  1955:44 mysqld
  571 nobody     20   0 14.740g 867004 565800 S   0.0 11.3 22:30:24 varnishd
24729 www-data   20   0  962100 132360  10524 R 100.0  1.7   0:02.61 apache2
24760 www-data   20   0  898276  62700   4680 R 100.0  0.8   0:00.62 apache2
24755 www-data   20   0  887024  56932   6476 R  19.1  0.7   0:00.57 apache2
24758 www-data   20   0  877304  47120   6632 R  28.7  0.6   0:00.62 apache2
24757 www-data   20   0  872980  40308   4300 R  86.0  0.5   0:00.30 apache2
24763 www-data   20   0  857388  25344   5604 R  19.1  0.3   0:00.04 apache2
24721 root       20   0  844416  13520   6704 S   0.0  0.2   0:00.03 apache2
  887 syslog     20   0  260268  12876    892 S   0.0  0.2   0:03.18 rsyslogd
```

You can see that MySQL is using the most memory at 54.8%. To see the actual amount of memory used in gigabytes, look at the RES column.

10.2. Monitoring Disk Usage

I use the *iotop* utility to monitor disk usage. This utility has to be installed by the user. To do so, type the following command on the command line:

```
sudo apt-get install iotop
```

To start *iotop*, type:

```
sudo iotop
```

Here is what *iotop* looks like on a busy web server:

```
Total DISK READ :       0.00 B/s | Total DISK WRITE :      33.51 M/s
Actual DISK READ:       0.00 B/s | Actual DISK WRITE:     611.54 K/s
  TID  PRIO  USER     DISK READ  DISK WRITE  SWAPIN     IO>    COMMAND
27393 be/4 mysql      0.00 B/s  572.08 K/s   0.00 %   0.57 % mysqld
  222 be/3 root       0.00 B/s    0.00 B/s   0.00 %   0.37 % [jbd2/xvda1-8]
27380 be/4 mysql      0.00 B/s    0.00 B/s   0.00 %   0.05 % mysqld
 6662 be/4 nobody     0.00 B/s    3.95 K/s   0.00 %   0.00 % varnishd ~re.bin,14G
 6664 be/4 nobody     0.00 B/s.   3.95 K/s   0.00 %   0.00 % varnishd ~re.bin,14G
  579 be/4 nobody     0.00 B/s    3.95 K/s   0.00 %   0.00 % varnishd ~re.bin,14G
 6666 be/4 nobody     0.00 B/s   19.73 K/s   0.00 %   0.00 % varnishd ~re.bin,14G
 2656 be/4 nobody     0.00 B/s    3.95 K/s   0.00 %   0.00 % varnishd ~re.bin,14G
 8870 be/4 mysql      0.00 B/s    0.00 B/s   0.00 %   0.00 % mysqld
29390 be/4 nobody     0.00 B/s    3.95 K/s   0.00 %   0.00 % varnishd ~re.bin,14G
 6659 be/4 nobody     0.00 B/s   19.73 K/s   0.00 %   0.00 % varnishd ~re.bin,14G
 6661 be/4 nobody     0.00 B/s   15.78 K/s   0.00 %   0.00 % varnishd ~re.bin,14G
24640 be/4 nobody     0.00 B/s    7.89 K/s   0.00 %   0.00 % varnishd ~re.bin,14G
12237 be/4 nobody     0.00 B/s   11.84 K/s   0.00 %   0.00 % varnishd ~re.bin,14G
 7642 be/4 nobody     0.00 B/s   11.84 K/s   0.00 %   0.00 % varnishd ~re.bin,14G
    1 be/4 root       0.00 B/s    0.00 B/s   0.00 %   0.00 % init
```

The first line of the utility is the most interesting, as it shows total disk read and write. If your site is slow and CPU usage is slow, you can come into *iotop* to see if there is some process that is hogging the disk's read or write capacity.

10.3. Monitoring Network Usage

The simplest tool for monitoring what is coming in and going out of your server is *ifstat*. It helps you get a quick idea of your server's bandwidth usage:

```
root@ip-10-168-72-176:/home/ubuntu# ifstat
      eth0
KB/s in  KB/s out
  29.19    222.07
  22.21    176.02
  23.02    190.54
  18.42    105.00
  16.81    140.57
 189.53    272.56
 576.14    620.53
```

10.4. Monitoring Apache for Crashes and Auto-Restarting It

Apache can be quite crash-prone when handling complex high-traffic websites. If you care about avoiding downtime on your websites, it is essential that you have away of monitoring Apache's status and restarting it when it crashes.

Luckily, it is quite simple to implement a monitoring and auto-restart mechanism. Create a file in your home directory named *apache_monitor.sh*. First, go to your home directory using the *cd* command:

```
cd
```

Typing "cd" alone, without specifying where you want to go, takes you to your home directory.

Next, create the file:

```
touch apache_monitor.sh
```

Since this file is going to be a script, it requires execution permissions, given to it as follows:

```
chmod +x apache_monitor.sh
```

Since you are inside your home directory, you do not need to use *sudo*.

Open up the file for editing, and paste this stuff inside it, updating the domain name and email address to your own:

```
#!/bin/bash
if curl -s --head http://example.com/?t=`date +%s` | grep "200 OK" > /dev/null
  then
    echo "The server is up!" > /dev/null
  else
    service apache2 restart
    mail -s "Server Notification" myemail@example.com <<< "Server restarted due to unreachability."
fi
```

This is a "shell script". It uses the *curl* tool to request a page on your site. It appends a timestamp to the request (made up of the number of seconds since January 1, 1970) to make Varnish think it is always requesting a new page. For example, it may request this page when you run it right now:

```
http://example.com/?t=1456002583
```

If you run it a few seconds later, it will request this page instead:

```
http://example.com/?t=1456002587
```

To Varnish, these are two different pages, so it never offers a cached page. To Apache, they are both requests for the home page, since the stuff after the domain is preceded by a question mark, which is special syntax for sending a variable to a server.

Anyway, what this means is that this is a perfect way to check if your server is up, as the script requests a fresh page from your server, and if the server doesn't correctly respond to the request, the script restarts Apache and also sends you an email to notify you. If the server is up, nothing is done. The message "The server is up!" is actually never seen by anyone since it is directed into */dev/null*, which in the Linux world means the output is being thrown into the void.

To make this script run automatically every minute 24/7, you'd create a "cron job" for it. Here's what you need to do. Type this in the command line:

```
sudo crontab -e
```

If this is your first time using *crontab*, you will be prompted to choose an editor. Press the number of the editor that you like on the list that you are offered, then press Enter.

You will be shown the *crontab* file, which on a fresh install is empty except for comments. Add this line to the very bottom of the file:

```
* * * * * /home/ubuntu/apache_monitor.sh >/dev/null 2>&1
```

Save the file and exit. Now, the operating system will call *apache_monitor.sh* every minute, which will request a webpage from your server. If the page loads fine, nothing happens. If it doesn't load for whatever reason, Apache is restarted and you get an email.

I have never had a need to restart Varnish except when modifying its configuration files. It can run for months without issue. The same is true for MySQL. Generally when there is a problem, it is either Apache (perhaps because somebody is hitting your site with tons of requests so that Apache runs out of memory or runs into some other error), or the disk is full.

11

Building a Server Farm and Load Balancing it with Varnish

In this chapter, I will show you how to create a small server farm made up of a Varnish load balancer, multiple Apache-specific server, and one powerful MySQL server. Scaling MySQL to multiple servers is a difficult and time-consuming and often painful task, and unless your database is so large that there is no server that offers enough RAM to hold it, you should go with a single MySQL server. Currently the largest AWS instance interms of memory offers 244 gigabytes of RAM. If your database is less than this size, you should probably go with a single instance.

11.1. Creating the Varnish Instance

To start off, create a new instance on which you will run Varnish as the load balancer. Use a T2 Nano instance for this, which costs less than $5/month to run. The T2 Nano instance has only one core and low network throughput, but it should easily handle 50,000-100,000 visitors per day for most sites, since Varnish uses very litte CPU, and unless people are constantly downloading large files (10-100 megabytes) from the server, the network bandwidth shouldn't be an issue. Testing, of course, is essential, and if the T2 Nano cannot handle your particular needs, you can change it to a T2 Micro (the next tier up) in minutes.

Note: Make sure to launch all your instances into the same availability zone to avoid high network latency.

Create the instance using the same steps used at the beginning of this book. On Step 4 ("Add Storage"), make sure to add enough storage to hold the Varnish cache. Since T2 Nano instances have only 500M of memory, use the file-based caching option with Varnish, which means that Varnish will store cached webpages on disk, while also allowing the operating system to hold the most accessed webpages in whatever free RAM that is available.

On Step 6 ("Configure Security Group"), make sure to enable both ports 22 and 80 and set the "Source" for both to "Anywhere". It is better to reuse an existing security group rather than letting Amazon create a new one for you, since in the future if you want to open a particular port on all your servers, you will only have one security group to update.

Step 6: Configure Security Group

A security group is a set of firewall rules that control the traffic for your instance. On this page, you can add rules to allow specific traffic to reach your instance. For example, if you want to set up a web server and allow Internet traffic to reach your instance, add rules that allow unrestricted access to the HTTP and HTTPS ports. You can create a new security group or select from an existing one below. Learn more about Amazon EC2 security groups.

Assign a security group: ◎ Create a **new** security group

◉ Select an **existing** security group

Filter VPC security groups ▼

Security Group ID	Name	Description	Actions
sg-ae3b95c8	default	default VPC security group	Copy to new
sg-c03896a6	launch-wizard-2	launch-wizard-2 created 2015-10-28T14:15:52.500-05:00	Copy to new
sg-10078969	launch-wizard-3	launch-wizard-3 created 2016-01-08T12:10:10.110-05:00	Copy to new

Go through the rest of the wizard until you are done launching your instance. The server will also require configuration, which we will deal with pretty soon.

11.2. Creating the MySQL Instance

For the MySQL instance, use a T2 Medium instance, which has four gigabytes of memory. Instead of launching a new instance, take a snapshot of the existing instance which has your MySQL data on it and launch an instance from that.

To do so, first you need to "stop" (turn off) the instance, done by right-clicking the instance's name, pointing to "Instance State" and then clicking on "Stop".

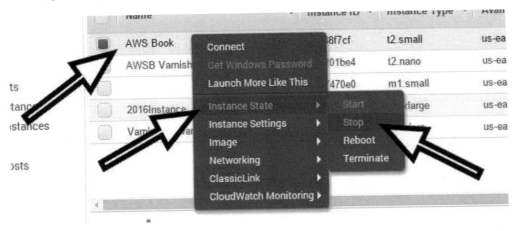

Once it has stopped, right-click on the instance's name again, point to "Image" and click "Create Image". You are creating a "machine image" (which Amazon calls an AMI, for "Amazon Machine Image"), which is why it uses the word "image".

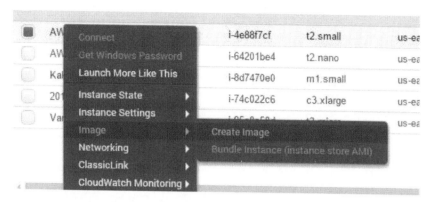

In the dialog box that opens, give the image a name and leave the rest of the settings alone. Then click "Create Image":

The dialog box closes. To monitor the progress of the image creation process, click "Snapshots" on the EC2 left menu.

You will see a progress bar next to your image name. If it stays at 0% for too long, click your browser's refresh/reload button and you may see that the image creation is actually finished. The process will take longer for larger disks.

Once it is done, click on AMIs on the left menu.

Right click on your image's name and click "Launch".

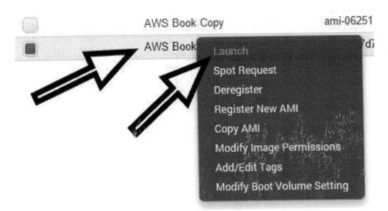

The AWS instance creation wizard will open up. Choose the instance type, which is going to be a T2 Medium (unless you have something else in mind), then click "Next: Configure Instance Details".

	Family	Type	vCPUs ⓘ	Memory (GiB)	Instance Storage (GB) ⓘ	EBS-Optimized Available ⓘ	Network Performance ⓘ
☐	General purpose	t2.nano	1	0.5	EBS only	-	Low to Moderate
☐	General purpose Free tier eligible	t2.micro	1	1	EBS only	-	Low to Moderate
☐	eral purpose	t2.small	1	2	EBS only	-	Low to Moderate
■	General purpose	t2.medium	2	4	EBS only	-	Low to Moderate
☐	General purpose	t2.large	2	8	EBS only	-	Low to Moderate
☐	General purpose	m4.large	2	8	EBS only	Yes	Moderate
☐	General purpose	m4.xlarge	4	16	EBS only	Yes	High
☐	General purpose	m4.2xlarge	8	32	EBS only		High

Cancel   Previous   **Review and Launch**   Next: Configure Instance Details

Leave the settings as they are then click: "Next: Add Storage". Change the size of the disk to fit your needs. Note that the larger the size, the more bandwidth the disk will have. In the future, if your database is about to outgrow the disk, you can easily attach a larger disk to the instance and move the MySQL databases onto it without having to recreate the instance.

Step 4: Add Storage

Your instance will be launched with the following storage device settings. You can attach additional EBS volumes and instance store volumes to your instance, or edit the settings of the root volume. You can also attach additional EBS volumes after launching an instance, but not instance store volumes. Learn more about storage options in Amazon EC2.

Volume Type ⓘ	Device ⓘ	Snapshot ⓘ	Size (GiB) ⓘ	Volume Type ⓘ	IOPS ⓘ	Delete on Termination ⓘ	Encrypted ⓘ
Root	/dev/sda1	snap-aa65c2b7	20	General Purpose SSD (GP2) ▾	60 / 3000	☑	Not Encrypted

Add New Volume

Click "Next" until you reach the "Configure Security Group" page. Since this is not a web server but a database server, it will need different security settings. The server will need SSH access, therefore keep that. You will also need to open up a port to let your other servers access the database. The default MySQL port is 3306, but to protect the server from automated hacking attempts, use a different port (and remember it since your Apache servers will need to know the port. You can, of course, always look it up by going to the Instances page, clicking on the instance's name and browsing its details until you find the Security Groups section, then clicking on the link there.)

Below, I am opening up the port 27931 for MySQL.

Step 6: Configure Security Group

A security group is a set of firewall rules that control the traffic for your instance. On this page, you can add rules to allow specific traffic to reach your instance. For example, if you want to set up a web server and allow Internet traffic to reach your instance, add rules that allow unrestricted access to the HTTP and HTTPS ports. You can create a new security group or select from an existing one below. Learn more about Amazon EC2 security groups.

Assign a security group: ⦿ Create a **new** security group

◯ Select an **existing** security group

Security group name:

launch-wizard-4

Description:

launch-wizard-4 created 2016-02-20T19:52:22.862-05:00

Type ⓘ	Protocol ⓘ	Port Range ⓘ	Source ⓘ		
SSH ▾	TCP	22	Anywhere ▾	0.0.0.0/0	✕
Custom TCP Rule ▾	TCP	27931	Anywhere ▾	0.0.0.0/0	✕

Add Rule

⚠ Warning
Rules with source of 0.0.0.0/0 allow all IP addresses to access your instance. We recommend setting security group rules to allow access from known IP addresses only.

Cancel   Previous   **Review and Launch**

Once you are ready, click "Review and Launch", then on the new page click "Launch". You will be prompted about key pairs, you can select your existing one so that you do not have to go through the PuTTYgen process all over again.

Before moving onto configuring the server, we will create the Apache instances just so that we have all instances we want before we start the configuration process.

11.3. Creating and Configuring the Apache Instances

You will use the pre-existing original instance as one of your Apache instances, then clone it twice until you have three servers. To avoid having to edit the same set of configuration files on three servers, you will first set up the original instance to work properly with the Varnish and MySQL instances, then clone it.

Log into the original instance and remove Varnish and MySQL using these commands:

```
sudo apt-get varnish remove
sudo apt-get remove mysql-server
sudo apt-get autoremove
```

The last line removes third-party libraries that were used by the two programs but that are no longer needed. Run these two commands to delete your MySQL databases and configuration files:

```
sudo rm -r /var/lib/mysql
sudo rm -r /etc/mysql
```

Navigate to */etc/apache2/sites-available* and update the virtualhost setting for each of your domains so that they use the port 80, rather than 8080. That is, change the top line of each .conf file (such as example.com.conf) from:

```
<VirtualHost *:8080>
```

to:

```
<VirtualHost *:80>
```

Next, update the */etc/apache2/ports.conf* file so that the top *Listen* directive is set as follows:

```
Listen 80
```

Now, it is time to prepare your WordPress installations to connect to the external MySQL server that you are going to set up. Open up */var/www/html/wordpress/wp-config.php* and update the DB_HOST configuration as follows:

```
/** MySQL hostname */ define('DB_HOST', '54.209.82.142:27931');
```

54.209.82.142 is the IP of the MySQL instance and 27931 is the MySQL port number that I chose in the security group earlier (later I will also have to configure MySQL to listen on this port). Note that the IP address and port name are separated by a colon.

That is all the configuration that is needed on the Apache instance for now. Later will do more to set up file replication between the Apache instance. For now, it is time to do the cloning.

11.4. Launching the Apache Instances

Previously we cloned the original instance to set up the MySQL instance. Now, we will delete that particular image (since we don't need it any more, is outdated, and it costs us money to store it) and create a new one to clone from.

To delete an image, go to the AMIs page, right click on the image's name, then click "Deregister".

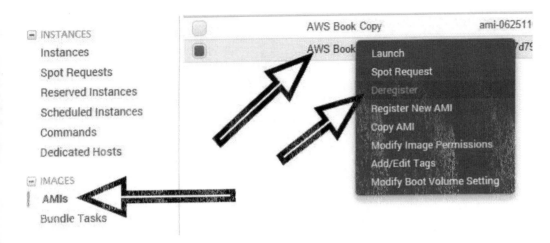

Next, click on Snapshots on the left menu, right click on the snapshot for the image and click "Delete".

Now, stop the Apache instance in your Instances page.

Once it is done stopping, right click on it, point to "Image" and click "Create Image" as you did for the MySQL instance.

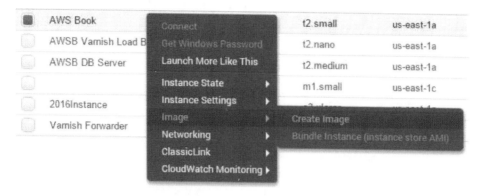

Once the snapshot is done, go to the AMIs page to find your image there.

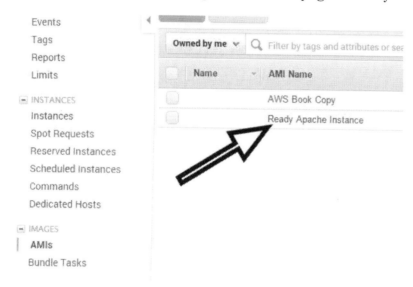

Right click on it and click "Launch". For the instance type I am choosing T2 Small, the same as the original instance.

One thing we will do differently from before is that on Step 3 you will choose to launch two instances, not one:

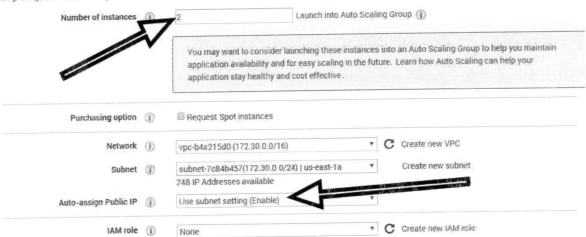

Also make sure that the "Auto-assign Public IP" setting is set to "Use subnet setting (Enable)" or "Enable", both of which do the same thing.

Go through the rest of the instance creation process. Make sure the security group allows access to port 80.

Once done, go back to your Instances page to see the instance launch progress:

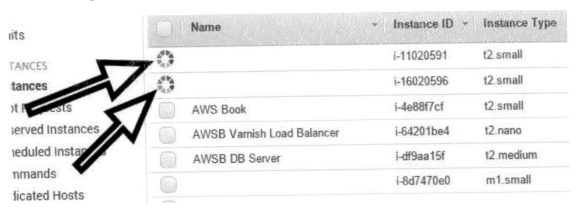

Give all three instances (the original and the two new ones) friendly names so that you can identify them easily:

The Apache instances are now ready. Later we will set up replication so that all three instances always have the same files (otherwise if you edit a WordPress theme in one of them, the other two will not reflect the change).

11.5. Configuring the Varnish Instance

If you used the same keypair for the Varnish Instance as you did for your earlier one, use these steps to quickly create a new profile for this instance in PuTTY by cloning the old profile, so that you do not need to browse to the location of the key file again.

Open PuTTY and click on the profile name of your original instance (assuming, of course, that you bothered to save a profile for it), then click "Load".

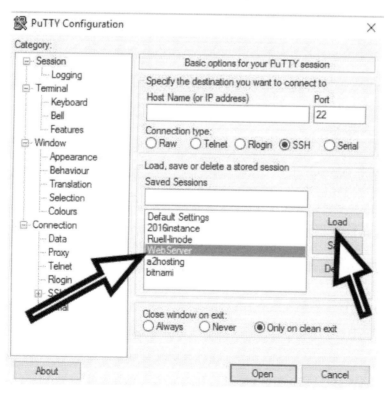

Next, paste your new instance's public IP address in the Host Name box, in the "Saved Sessions" box type a new name for your profile, then click "Save". This will create a new profile without overwriting the original server's profile, and it will have the same key file associated with it so that you do not have to worry about that.

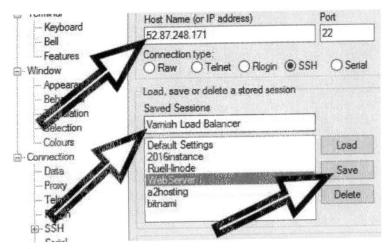

Once inside the Varnish instance, run the following commands to update Ubuntu and install Varnish:

sudo apt-get update; sudo apt-get upgrade; sudo apt-get install varnish

On the command line, for convenience you can type multiple commands in the shell and separate them by semicolons so that they are run one after another. They won't be run in parallel.

Check how much free disk space the server has left through the following command:

df -h

```
ubuntu@ip-172-30-0-127:~$ df -h
Filesystem      Size  Used Avail Use% Mounted on
udev            240M   12K  240M   1% /dev
tmpfs            49M  328K   49M   1% /run
/dev/xvda1       12G 1020M   11G   9% /
```

As can be seen, the server's root disk has 11 gigabytes of free space (the "Avail" column). We will give Varnish 10 gigabytes of disk space for its cache, so that one gigabyte remains for updates and any other future operations. In the future you can always easily set the Varnish cache to a different size if necessary.

To do so, first open up */etc/default/varnish* for editing and set the DAEMON_OPTS parameter as follows:

```
DAEMON_OPTS="-a :80 \
     -T localhost:6082 \
     -f /etc/varnish/default.vcl \
```

```
        -S /etc/varnish/secret \
        -s file,/varnish_storage.bin,10G"
```

Next, open up */etc/varnish/default.vcl*. Find the *backend* section, which is at the top of the file:

```
backend default {
    .host = "127.0.0.1";
    .port = "8080";
}
```

Remove that and put this instead:

```
backend apache_1 {
    .host = "52.86.4.143";
    .port = "80";
}
backend apache_2 {
    .host = "54.174.43.248";
    .port = "80";
}
backend apache_3 {
    .host = "52.87.190.9";
    .port = "80";
}
```

Update the IP addresses to reflect the IP addresses of your three Apache instances.

Then we will create a "director" that does the load balancing:

```
director default_director round-robin {
    { .backend = apache_1; }
    { .backend = apache_2; }
    { .backend = apache_3; }
}
```

And finally, we will add this line to the top of the *vcl_recv* function:

```
sub vcl_recv {
    set req.backend = default_director;
```

Restart Varnish. If it fails to restart and tells you "Servname not supported", you probably have an unnecessary space in one of your IP addresses.

If you are still using a test domain with your site (set up through your hosts file), you'd need to update the hosts file to refer to the Varnish instance's IP address.

11.6. Configuring the MySQL Instance

Log into your MySQL instance and open up */etc/mysql/my.cnf* and change the port number under the "client" section to your chosen MySQL port:

```
[client]
port       = 27931
```

Next, find the "mysqld" section and there too change the port number:

```
[mysqld]
#
# * Basic Settings
#
user        = mysql
pid-file    = /var/run/mysqld/mysqld.pid
socket      = /var/run/mysqld/mysqld.sock
port        = 27931
```

Find the bind-address directive and comment it out to disable it, i.e. if you find a line like this:

```
bind-address        = 127.0.0.1
```

Change it to this:

```
#bind-address        = 127.0.0.1
```

The # character turns the line into a "comment", which makes MySQL ignore it.

Now, log into the MySQL server as the root user using the MySQL client. Type this on the command line:

```
mysql -u root -p
```

Press Enter. You will be prompted for a password, type it in. Once inside, type this command then press Enter:

```
GRANT ALL PRIVILEGES ON wordpress.* TO wordpressuser@'%' identified by 'PASSWORD';
```

Make sure to update the above to reflect your particular settings. *wordpress.** refers to all the tables inside the *wordpress* database, which is a database we created at the beginning of this book. Some people may choose to name the database after their website, therefore when working on sites owned by others, in most cases this database will not be named *wordpress*. *wordpressuser* refers to the MySQL user that you created for WordPress. Update PASSWORD to reflect the password you chose for *wordpressuser*.

The above command tells MySQL to accept connections from the *wordpressuser* from any IP address. This is necessary since the MySQL server is going to be receiving connections from three different IP addresses (the three Apache instances).

Restart MySQL to tell it to start using the new settings:

```
sudo service mysql restart
```

This server is now ready to respond to database queries.

11.7. Testing the Server Farm

You are now ready to test your site. Type in the domain or the Varnish instance IP address in a browser and the WordPress site should load. If you get a 500 *timeout* error, it probably means your Varnish instance is unreachable for some reason. If you get a 503 Service Unavailable error, it means Varnish is reachable, but the Apache instances are not. If you get a database connection error, it means the MySQL instance is not reachable, perhaps because of a wrong setting in the *wp-config.php* file of the Apache instances, or because of a security group issue or wrong configuration on the MySQL instance.

If everything goes smoothly, you will see the your WordPress site and in the Network tab of the Firefox inspector, you will see the familiar Varnish headers (see section 8.7 for more details on viewing the Varnish headers in Firefox).

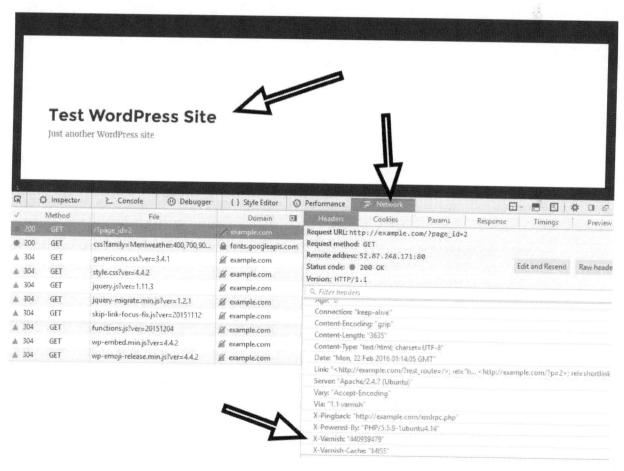

11.8. Identifying the Instance that a Webpage is Loaded From

It is important to make sure that all the instances are correctly responding to requests, and to do this, you can make Varnish send an extra header that identifies the back-end Apache instance that responded to the request.

Luckily this is quite simple to do. Log into the Varnish instance and open up /etc/varnish/default.vcl, then add this line to the *vcl_fetch* function:

```
set req.http.Farm-Worker = beresp.backend.name;
```

This is telling Varnish to create a custom HTTP header named *Farm-Worker*, and the content of the header should be the name of the backend server. We set the name at the top of the file where we wrote the backend directives and specified the IP and port of the backend servers, in our example we used *apache_1*, *apache_2* and *apache_3* to name our backend instances. Here we are basically setting a variable, to be retrieved in the function described next.

Next, edit the *vcl_deliver* function so that it looks like this:

```
sub vcl_deliver {
    if(obj.hits > 0) {
        set resp.http.X-Varnish-Cache = "HIT ("+obj.hits+")";
        set resp.http.Farm-Worker = req.http.Farm-Worker;
    } else {
        set resp.http.X-Varnish-Cache = "MISS";
        set resp.http.Farm-Worker = req.http.Farm-Worker;
    }
}
```

Here, we are setting the *response* headers to include the *Farm-Worker* header, which we are retrieving from the *request* headers that we set earlier.

Save and close the file, then restart Varnish. Now, when you visit your site, you will see the *Farm-Worker* directive in the Firefox Headers pane:

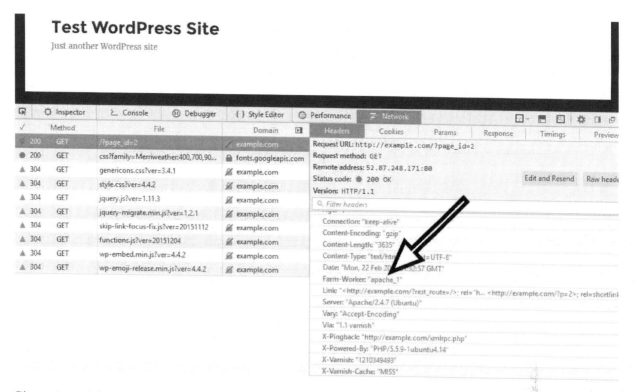

Since Varnish caches pages, it makes a back-end request only when requesting an uncached page. If the page you are visiting has already been cached, then there is no Apache involvement since the webpage was served by Varnish with no reference to the Apache instances. Therefore if you keep refreshing the same page, you will keep getting the same backend server name in the *Farm-Worker* header, since that server was actually called only once and it is not being called again when you reload the page. To see if all the servers are responding to requests, you'd need to keep browsing to new, uncached pages. A simple way of doing this is to append a *query string* to the end of your domain name, as follows:

example.com?1

We have already covered a use of query strings in section 10.4 when we set up the script to auto-restart Apache on crashes. This makes Varnish think you are requesting a new page, while it actually just goes to your home page. To do the next test, type

example.com?2

On typing the above, I was able to receive the web page from the *apache_2* server:

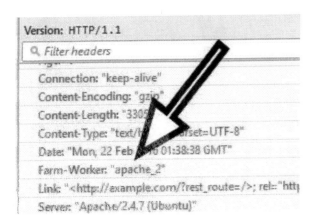

And on typing:

```
example.com?3
```

I see that *apache_3* responded to the request. Since we are using the *round-robin* director for the Varnish load balancer, the first request will go to the first server, the second to the second, the third to the third, and the fourth back to the first, and so on. Varnish also offers the *random* directory (just change the word *round-robin* to *random* in the *default.vcl* file), which randomly distributes load among the backend servers.

12

Setting Up Cross Replication between the Apache Instances

When you have multiple Apache instances serving the same files, it is essential that there is a replication solution to keep the instances in sync, other when you or a user makes a change to one of the site's files, the change will not be reflected on the other servers. And when you make a configuration change on one of the servers, you'd have to manually update the other two as well.

We are going to be syncing the WordPress installations and the Apache configuration files. What we need to do is set up cross replication, which is a specific type of replication that needs specific tools. The *rsync* tool is great when you need to copy data from a main server to a backup server. But it doesn't work if you need to copy data both ways between two servers. What we need is *unison*, the Linux cross replication tool.

What we will do is set up cross replication between Server 1 and Server 2, then set up cross replication between Server 1 and Server 3.

12.1. Setting Up the Private Keys

To set up key-based access between the instances for replication, you need to set up your private keys on the servers, which *unison* will use when connecting from one server to another. Log into the first Apache server. In your home directory, go into the *.ssh* directory which is a hidden directory that holds SSH settings for a particular user.

```
cd .ssh
```

Then create a file called anything you like, such as *ubuntu_user_private_key.pem*, and open it up for editing:

```
sudo touch ubuntu_user_private_key.pem
sudo nano ubuntu_user_private_key.pem
```

Here you will need the .pem file that you downloaded from Amazon when you created your first instance (assuming you have been using the same key pair since then for all of your instances, if you haven't, you'd use the .pem file for the second instance here, and you'd also need to add another file for the private key of the third instance).

Open up the file you just created, and open up the .pem file on your computer. Copy the contents of the .pem file into *ubuntu_user_private_key.pem*. If you are using PuTTY, you can paste by right-clicking on the PuTTY window.

Next, change the file's permissions to make them more restrictive, otherwise the system will not let you use the private key:

```
sudo chmod 600 ubuntu_user_private_key.pem
```

Repeat these steps on the remaining instances.

12.2. Setting up Permissions for the Ubuntu User

In order to use *unison* properly, the *ubuntu* user (the user we have been using to log in to the servers) needs to have write permissions on the directories and files that we want to sync.

The first thing is to add the *ubuntu* user to the Apache group (*www-data*):

```
sudo adduser ubuntu www-data
```

Next, we will update the directories we want to sync to be more permissive toward group members:

```
sudo find /var/www -type d -exec chmod 775 {} \;
sudo find /var/www -type f -exec chmod 664 {} \;
sudo find /etc/apache2 -type d -exec chmod 775 {} \;
sudo find /etc/apache2 -type f -exec chmod 664 {} \;
```

Then we will update the */etc/apache2* directory so that it is owned by the Apache group:

```
sudo chown -R root:www-data *
```

Do the above steps on all three instances.

12.3 Log Out and Log Back In

After making the changes in the previous section, it is necessary to log out and log back in so that the *ubuntu* user will start using the new group membership permissions. If you don't do that, the next few sections will not work as expected, therefore I might as well be extra cautious and make this its own section!

12.4. Installing and Testing Unison

Use the following command to install *unison*:

```
sudo apt-get install unison
```

After installing *unison* on all the servers, you can test that it is on and responding to remote requests by running the following command. In this example I am on Server 1 running this command to test Server 2:

```
sudo ssh -i /home/ubuntu/.ssh/ubuntu_user_private_key.pem ubuntu@54.174.43.248 unison –version
```

This should return the *unison* version on Server 2, which in my case is as follows:

unison version 2.40.102

Note that, as has already been mentioned, *ubuntu_user_private_key.pem* refers to the remote server's *ubuntu* user private key. The IP address in the command is also the remote server's IP. We are logging into the remote server as the *ubuntu* user and running the *unison –version* command on it. It doesn't matter what our local username is. It just so happens that the remote server's username and our own username is the same.

12.5. Setting up Unison Profiles

After installing *unison*, you should have a *.unison* directory in your home directory. We will only need to set up *unison* profiles on Apache 1, since we will use this server to manage all cross replication with the other servers.

The *.unison* This is where *unison* keeps its configurations. Go into this directory on the Apache 1 server:

cd /home/ubuntu/.unison

Copy the *default.prf* file and name the new file *apache1x2.prf*, as this will be the profile for cross replicating the Apache 1 and Apache 2 servers. We will later create an *apache1x3.prf* file to set up cross replication between Apache 1 and 3.

sudo cp default.prf apache1x2.prf

Open the *apache1x2.prf* file. It currently doesn't contain any configurations.

sudo nano apache1x2.prf

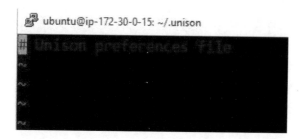

First, define the *unison* root directories. The actual directories that we will sync will be relative to these root directories. These root directories themselves will not by synced. In our case, since we are going to by syncing files from various areas of the filesystem, the root directories will have to be the server roots (the very top directory that you see when you type *cd /*)

root=/
root=ssh://ubuntu@52.86.4.143//

Above, we are telling *unison* that our local replication root is the top directory, while also saying that the remote replication root is also the top directory.

Next, we will define the SSH arguments necessary to connect from one server to another:

```
sshargs=-i /home/ubuntu/.ssh/ubuntu_user_private_key.pem
```

We are defining the private key of the remote server's user in the above line. We've already defined the username in the second *root* line (ubuntu@52.86.4.143), so we don't need to repeat it here. If Server 2's SSH port had been different from the default (22), you'd add *-port XXXX* to define the port on the *sshargs* line.

Now, it is time to tell *unison* what directories to replicate:

```
path = var/www/html
path = etc/apache2
```

You specify each path only once, it is assumed that they exist on both servers. Note that they are "relative" paths, which is why we are writing *etc* instead of the usual */etc*. We've already specified at the beginning that these paths are relative to /, therefore it is implicit that we mean */var* when we type *var*.

Since the replication is going to happen automatically without our supervision, we will need the following three lines to make things work smoothly:

```
batch = true
force= newer
```

batch tells *unison* to never prompt you for anything. *force= newer* tells *unison* to always prefer to keep the newer version of a file, regardless of which server it is from. This is important since we never know on which server a file is going to get changed, our only criterion for preferring one file over another is that it is newest version. This also makes file deletion work properly; if the newest "event" regarding a file is that it got deleted on Server 3, the deletion will get propagated to the other servers.

Here's my completed apache1x2.prf file, in case you wanted to see all the lines in one place:

```
root=/
root=ssh://ubuntu@52.86.4.143//
sshargs=-i /home/ubuntu/.ssh/ubuntu_user_private_key.pem
path = var/www/html
batch = true
force= newer
```

And we are done here! Now, copy the *apache1x2.prf* file into a new file named *apache1x3.prf*:

```
sudo cp apache1x2.prf apache1x3.prf
```

Open apache1x3.prf and make the necessary changes to it to make it work with the Apache 3 server.

12.6. Doing a Test Replication Run

On Apache 1, inside the *.unison* directory, type the following command:

```
sudo unison apache1x2.prf
```

If everything is set up correctly, you'd see the following output:

```
ubuntu@ip-172-30-0-53:~/.unison$ sudo unison apache1x2.prf
sudo: unable to resolve host ip-172-30-0-53
Contacting server...
Connected [//ip-172-30-0-15// -> //ip-172-30-0-53//]
Looking for changes
  Waiting for changes from server
Reconciling changes
Nothing to do: replicas have not changed since last sync.
```

Since the contents that we want to sync are exactly the same on both servers, nothing happens. After making a change to a theme file (*header.php*) on Apache 2 and a change to a theme file on Apache 1 (*functions.php*), we now get some interesting output:

```
ubuntu@ip-172-30-0-53:~/.unison$ sudo unison apache1x2.prf
sudo: unable to resolve host ip-172-30-0-53
Contacting server...
Connected [//ip-172-30-0-15// -> //ip-172-30-0-53//]
Looking for changes
  Waiting for changes from server
Reconciling changes
changed   ---->            var/www/html/wordpress/wp-content/themes/twentysixteen
/functions.php
local        : changed file      modified on 2016-03-02 at  1:50:42  size 14258
     rw-rw-r--
ip-172-30... : unchanged file     modified on 2016-01-06 at 18:31:30  size 14251
     rw-rw-r--
          <---- changed    var/www/html/wordpress/wp-content/themes/twentysixteen
/header.php
local        : unchanged file     modified on 2016-03-02 at  1:42:48  size 4322
     rw-rw-r--
ip-172-30... : changed file      modified on 2016-03-02 at  1:50:44  size 4336
     rw-rw-r--
Propagating updates
UNISON 2.40.102 started propagating changes at 01:50:59.83 on 02 Mar 2016
[BGN] Updating file var/www/html/wordpress/wp-content/themes/twentysixteen/funct
ions.php from / to //ip-172-30-0-15//
[BGN] Updating file var/www/html/wordpress/wp-content/themes/twentysixteen/heade
r.php from //ip-172-30-0-15// to /
[END] Updating file var/www/html/wordpress/wp-content/themes/twentysixteen/funct
ions.php
[END] Updating file var/www/html/wordpress/wp-content/themes/twentysixteen/heade
r.php
UNISON 2.40.102 finished propagating changes at 01:50:59.84 on 02 Mar 2016
Saving synchronizer state
Synchronization complete at 01:50:59  (2 items transferred, 0 skipped, 0 failed)
```

On line 8 you see *changed* with an arrow pointing outward. It means a change is detected that needs to be pushed to the remote server. Down from there we see an arrow pointing inward with *changed* after it, this means a change has been detected on the remote server that needs to be pulled into the local server. Then we will see messages about the changes being carried out.

12.7. Automating the Replication Process

We've already covered using *cron* to automate tasks in section 10.4. When automating replication, it is best to ensure that the replication between Apache 1 and 2 doesn't happen at the same time as the replication between Apache 1 and 3. This will avoid unpredictable behavior when two instances of *unison* try to replicate from one server (Apache 1) to two outward servers (Apache 2 and 3). Avoiding this condition is as simple as creating a shell script and putting each *unison* command on its own line. The first line will get executed, and once it is done, the second line will get executed.

On Apache 1, create a file in your home directory named *unison_manager.sh*, then put this stuff in it:

```
#!/bin/bash
sudo unison apache1x2.prf
sudo unison apache1x3.prf
```

You shouldn't specify the path to the apache1x2.prf and the other profile file, since *unison* knows to look for it in the *.unison* directory of your user.

Save and close the file, then give it execute permissions:

```
sudo chmod +x unison_manager.sh
```

And now, open the *crontab* file:

```
sudo crontab -e
```

and add this to it:

```
* * * * * flock -n /tmp/lockfile /home/ubuntu/unison_manager.sh >/dev/null 2>&1
```
The * * * * * tells *cron* to run this task every minute. *flock* (f-lock, i.e. file lock) is a Linux utility that in the above command helps us avoid running *unison_manager.sh* if it is already running. In the rare case that a synchronization between two servers takes more than a minute, this helps avoid having another instance of *unison_manager.sh* get called and start a new synchornization task that competes and perhaps messes up the already running synchronization task.

The */tmp/lockfile* is a file that *flock* needs in order to be able to do its thing. This file can be located anywhere and named anything. As long as *flock* can write to it, you are good to go.

That's it. We are done. The three servers will continue to replicate among themselves for ever and ever with no need for supervision.

12.8. Updating the Apache Auto-Restart Script to Work with Multiple Servers

If you remember from chapter 10, we wrote a script to auto-restart Apache. The script requested a page from our website, and if it failed to load, Apache would get restarted. But now that we have three servers, how do we tell which particular Apache is unreachable so that we can restart it?

It turns out it is pretty simple to do this. First, log into the Varnish instance. Then add the following to the bottom of the *vcl_recv* function:

```
if(req.url ~ "__apache_1") {
    set req.backend = apache_1;
}
if(req.url ~ "__apache_2") {
    set req.backend = apache_2;
```

```
    }
    if(req.url ~ "__apache_3") {
        set req.backend = apache_3;
    }
```

This is telling Varnish that if a request has __*apache_1* (that is two underscores before *apache*) in it, to send it to the *apache_1* instance, and so on for the other two instances. In othe words, when you type *example.com?__apache_1* in your browser, Varnish will always serve the site to you from the Apache 1 instance.

Next, we need to update the */home/ubuntu/apache_monitor.sh* script on each of the instances. Open it up on Apache 1 and change this:

```
if curl -s --head http://example.com/?t=`date +%s`
```

to this:

```
if curl -s --head http://example.com/?__apache_1&t=`date +%s`
```

This way, we are sending the __*apache_1* variable with the request (ensuring the Apache 1 backend is used), along with the timestamp (ensuring we are always served a fresh page rather than a cached page).

Now, open the *crontab* file:

```
sudo crontab -e
```

and make sure the *apache_monitor.sh* job is there. Notice that if you open *crontab* without using *sudo*, you will get a different *crontab* file (specific to the *ubuntu* user). With *sudo*, you will get the root user's *crontab*.

Since we cloned the instances, the *apache_monitor.sh* cron job should be there on all the instances, but it is good to make sure.

Update the *apache_monitor.sh* script on the remaining two instances, updating the aforementioned lines to use __*apache_2* and __*apache_3* respectively.

12.9. How to Edit Your Website's Files in a Replication Environment

When making edits to your website(s), it is best to do them on one of the servers and to have the changes propagate from this server to the rest. To do so, simple edit your *hosts* file so that it refers to the IP of one of the Apache servers (rather than the Varnish server). In this way, whenever you load *example.com*, it will always be from the server you specified. See section 5.1 for more details on using the *hosts* file.

Conclusion

I have shown you how to build a rudimentary high-performance web server set up. This is just the beginning. There are various improvements that can be added to increase performance and security.

If your websites are going to be hosting sensitive data (for example credit card information, social security numbers), it is essential you read a number of books on server security.

You'd also need to look into a backup solution. You can use the information in chapter 12 to set up a backup instance that uses *unison* or *rsync* to copy files over, and that uses *mysqldump* to backup the MySQL instance's data. You can use *cron* to automate the backup process, and use shell scripts to manage the backup files, deleting backups that are older than a certain date, since you do not have infinite storage.

My goal as a technical writer has always been to make technology easy and accessible to everyone who needs it. I hope I have accomplished some small part of this goal in writing this book.

Made in the USA
San Bernardino, CA
01 January 2018